FOLKTALES OF *Israel*

 *Folktales*
OF THE WORLD

GENERAL EDITOR : RICHARD M. DORSON

FOLKTALES OF
Israel

EDITED BY
Dov Noy
WITH THE ASSISTANCE OF
DAN BEN-AMOS

TRANSLATED BY
GENE BAHARAV

FOREWORD BY
RICHARD M. DORSON

THE UNIVERSITY OF CHICAGO PRESS

The University of Chicago Press, Chicago 60637
The University of Chicago Press, Ltd., London

© 1963 *by The University of Chicago. All rights reserved*
Published 1963. Printed in the United States of America

81 80 79 78 77   8 7 6 5 4

Paper   ISBN: 0-226-59720-2
LCN: 63-16721

Foreword

Both the oldest and the newest of folklore traditions are found in Israel. As a young nation-state, created in 1948, where European, Asiatic, African, and American immigrants mingle with Palestinian natives, Israel is just developing her national character. But the Jewish-biblical lore that unites and has brought together the heterogeneous Israelis harks back to the oldest records of Western civilization.

Hence, when we speak of the folklore of Israel, we refer both to the oral legend and parable and metaphor which express many facets of the Jewish popular faith and to the variegated bodies of tales and songs, customs and beliefs brought into Israel by her immigrants. Or, phrased another way, the people of Israel relate narratives peculiar to Jewish religious tradition, and they tell international tales belonging to the same general stock known from India to Ireland. In the first category fall wandering fictions of the kind found in the Grimms' collection of Household Tales. Both these story-groups appear in the present volume.

Among the Jewish people the telling of stories and the learning of the faith are interwoven in a manner unparalleled in other countries of Western civilization. The Old Testament itself freezes into scripture one set of creation and origin myths and the epic deeds of primeval culture heroes. Within its books are revealed the penchant of Hebrew kings and prophets for relating moralistic tales and parables and proverbs based on stories. A special word, *mashal,* denoted these allegorical fictions. Then the Talmud, assembling the civil and canon law of the Hebrews in the fifth and sixth centuries A.D., recorded a host of legends gathered about the patriarchs and sages. From postbiblical times through the Middle Ages a large body of legalistic commentary and interpretation of the Old Testament, known as the Midrash, also included the written record of oral traditions, or Haggada. Haggadic legends illustrated the moral courage and supernatural wisdom of Abraham, David, Solomon, and other spiritual heroes. Sages of these olden times specialized in Agadoth, the telling of biblical stories which were then written down and brought together in edifying collections of rabbinical lore. In recent times the custom yet persists. The emergence in the eighteenth century in eastern Europe of a new sect of pious Jewry, the Hasidim, has brought in its wake a flood of legends celebrating the miraculous gifts of holy men. These Hasidic legendary tales are today told in Brooklyn by Yiddish-speaking immigrants from eastern Europe.

A curious reversal of the usual folklore process has thus transpired among the Jewish people, for the medium of written literature and the teachings of the rabbis have encouraged rather than suppressed the oral tradition. This situation creates perplexing problems for the folklorist who seeks to establish the continuity and independence of unwritten and non-learned traditions. To these problems eminent Jewish scholars addressed themselves.

The great Jewish folklorists, like Moses Gaster and Louis Ginzberg, devoted their energies to disentangling the Haggadic legends from the talmudic-midrashic literature and the myriad sources upon which it drew. Gaster (1856–1939) left Rumania for England in 1885, serving as chief rabbi of the Sephardic community there and attaining scholastic honors; in 1907 and 1908 he was elected president of the Folk-Lore Society. In the Society's memoir series he published *Rumanian Bird and Beast Stories* (1915), translating them from oral texts and providing a lengthy, learned introduction in which he theorized that religious sects in Syria and Byzantium had fathered these animal fables. In the realm of postbiblical Jewish legend, his chief contributions were two skilfully edited works, constantly cited in the comparative notes of the present volume. *The Exempla of the Rabbis* (1924) brought together four hundred fifty moralistic tales and anecdotes from fugitive Hebrew manuscript and printed sources extending over a span of fifteen hundred years. Gaster synopsized the tales in English and appended to them detailed notes indicating parallel examples. The *Ma'aseh Book* (subtitled *Book of Jewish Tales and Legends* [1934]), was, on the other hand, his translation from "Judeo-German" of a single collection of rabbinical tales published in Basel in 1602 by one Jacob ben Abraham. In the two hundred fifty-four texts, ranging from pious talmudic stories to marvelous fictions, Gaster beheld a veritable "Gesta Judaeorum," a counterpart of the famous *Gesta Romanorum*, which had assembled the most popular medieval legends of secular kings and Christian heroes. Literally, "Ma'aseh" means a story or event, and the *Ma'aseh Book* is thus a Jewish medley of old wives' tales.

In recent years Gaster's reputation as an Agadic scholar has suffered; for example, he considered the *Book of Exempla* the oldest work of the Hebrew Haggada, when it is actually a late collection. But his fame as a comparative folklorist continues to grow. Gaster knew the tale repertoires of Eastern and Western peoples, of the literary and spoken traditions, of the religious and secular worlds. Growing up in Rumania, he had occasion to hear the "nurse from Hungary, and the housemaid from Wallachia, the Albanian with his sweetmeats, and the peasant with his fowls and eggs, the pilgrim from the Holy Land, and the hawker, the Gipsy," each telling their store of tales or forming an animated circle around the garden gate to exchange their fictions. In his theoretical essays, Gaster commented astutely on the continuous interchange between written and oral versions of popular legends and on the folk process that converted saints' legends into fairy tales. In illustration, he cited folk accounts of the Virgin Mary. Some showed her as a "bad-tempered, evil-tongued, nasty woman" akin to the malevolent witch, and others as a benefactress who assisted the despairing with her conjurations and charms. From his personal knowledge and erudition, Gaster declared that the folktales of western Europe had lost their religious element still so prominent in the "incomparably richer" popular mythology of the eastern countries. This perspective makes Gaster a fitting commentator on the international tales borne by Jewish people.[1]

[1] Moses Gaster, *Studies and Texts in Folklore, Magic, Medieval Romance, Hebrew Apocrypha and Samaritan Archaeology* (3 vols.; London: Maggs Bros., 1925–28), II, 909–10, 911, 1097–98.

In furnishing his copious comparative references to the *Ma'aseh Book*, Gaster was assisted, particularly with the later narratives, by Louis Ginzberg (1873–1953), who had already produced his magisterial work, *The Legends of the Jews*. Ginzberg left Russia, the country of his birth, after advanced studies at German universities to reside in the United States from 1902 until his death. As professor of Talmud and of Rabbinics at the Jewish Theological Seminary in New York, he became the foremost rabbinical scholar of his generation, specializing in the Haggada, the subject of an early series of monographs he began to write in 1899. From this laborious investigation in half-a-dozen tongues of the Middle East and Europe emerged his inspirational idea—the orderly arrangement of Jewish biblical traditions, scattered in a thousand different hiding places, to parallel the narrative of the Old Testament. Somewhat in the fashion that Elias Lönnrot had strung together Finnish folk verses, charms, and legends into the smooth-flowing national epic of the *Kalevala,* Ginzberg selected and arranged his hard-won texts to render visible the religious folk epic of the Jews. The first four volumes of *The Legends of the Jews* (1910–13) presented a running narration of all biblical figures known in oral lore, from the Creation through Exodus and the lives of Moses and other great prophets. Two volumes of notes were issued in 1925 and 1928, and an index volume in 1938.

Ginzberg's *Legends* imposes a pattern on the Haggada that never existed in actuality. It is literally a work of creative scholarship. Because of space limitations and consideration for the reader, Ginzberg printed only one variant for each folk-biblical legend, although his notes lead the way to others. The fluent rendering of the narrative achieves originality by avoiding both the apocryphal and the agadic styles. Even the Haggada is an artificial construct, for, as Ginzberg recognized, the tellers of old traditions would not themselves draw a hard and fast line between the kernel of Jewish lore in the Haggada and the peripheral stories of the pseudepigrapha and apocrypha, which had been ruled out of bounds by the rabbinical fathers.

Writing in praise of his master's great work, a student of Ginzberg's has commented as follows.

> The design of the work is all his own, new and unconventional, no one before having thought of reshaping the Haggadah according to a pattern of Biblical events and personages. His predecessors in the field were satisfied merely to compile the scattered and dispersed folklore of their people into motley anthologies, performing hardly any greater service than making its perusal and study more convenient. Professor Ginzberg, on the other hand, recognizing in the welter of homiletical and fictitious material in which the *Talmudim* and *Midrashim* abound the protoplasm of organic creations . . . took the task of the student of the Haggadah to be the combining of the cells. . . . He traced out in the Haggadah the grand themes of the Bible and its more illustrious men and women. . . .[2]

Yet the very virtues here extolled must at the same time be regarded with caution by the folklorist. The "motley anthologies," while less imaginative and dramatic, are still closer in content and manner to folk expression than is an organic, symmetrical whole. For the folklorist, the great achievement of Ginzberg's masterwork is its documentary source material from which he culled the heart of Jewish folk tradition from the non-Jewish infiltrations and associations.

Ginzberg himself was a sophisticated folklore scholar in the broadest international sense, and he knew exactly what kinds of materials he was handling. He realized that Jewish people transmitted both their own and non-Jewish legends, fairy tales, fables, and anecdotes, and that Moslems and Christians and Christianized Africans related Jewish biblical legends. Still he could draw a boundary around the core of Hebrew religious folklore, as it came to full strength in ancient Israel and Babylonia before the destruction of the Temple. In a brilliant essay on "Jewish Folklore: East and West," delivered at the Harvard Tercentennial Celebration in 1936, Ginzberg marked out this central core and illustrated the borrowings, accretions, and exchanges between Jewish and Middle Eastern–European–Christian bodies of tradition. He

[2] Solomon Goldman, "The Portrait of a Teacher," in *Louis Ginzberg: Jubilee Volume on the Occasion of His Seventieth Birthday* (New York: American Academy for Jewish Research, 1945), p. 5.

saw Greece rather than India as the wellspring of Jewish-biblical folk themes; he recognized the folk emulation of Jewish prophets in the popular lore of Christian saints; he acknowledged the intrusion of pagan and Christian legends into the Haggada.[3]

For all his learning in and sensitivity to the nature of Jewish religious folk-narrative, Ginzberg still, like Gaster, worked only with the written versions of oral traditions. The fieldwork of Yehude-Leyb Cahan (1881–1937), the best known of a group of east European collectors active at the turn of the century, marks a departure in Jewish folklore studies. Born in Vilna, Poland, Cahan grew up in Warsaw, supporting himself as a watchmaker and jeweler but devoting his main energies to the folklore movement, which attracted nationalistically minded young Jewish intellectuals. On moving to London in 1901 and New York in 1904, where he remained until his death, Cahan continued to collect songs and tales from east European immigrants. He worked closely with the Yiddish Scientific Institute, or Yivo, established in 1925 with headquarters in Vilna and, after World War II, in New York, and edited their folklore publications. Two volumes of Yiddish folksongs he had collected appeared in 1912 and immediately became a standard work of reference.

The great projected edition of Cahan's collections of a thousand folklore texts, which was to have been published by Yivo in six volumes, was well under way in 1939 when the Germans occupied Poland and destroyed the holdings of Yivo. Only the folktale volume, *Yidishe folksmayses,* saw print in 1940. To its fifty-six tales can be added thirty-nine others discovered in manuscript in the Yivo archives in New York. Fortunately, the material for another proposed volume to be edited by Cahan had been shipped to New York, and *Studies in Yiddish Folklore (Shtudyes vegn yidisher folksshafung)* was published by Yivo in 1952. The essays in this work range over a variety of theoretical questions central to the tasks of the folklorist, with, of course, special application to Yiddish and Jewish materials. Cahan himself wrote on such mat-

---

[3] Reprinted in L. Ginzberg, *On Jewish Law and Lore* (Cleveland and New York: Meridian Books, 1962), pp. 61–73, from *Independence, Convergence, and Borrowing in Institutions* (Cambridge, Mass.: Harvard University Press, 1937).

ters as "Folksong versus 'Folksy' Song," "On Yiddish Folktales," "On Jewish Jokes," and "Instructions for the Folklore Collector." Cahan revisited Vilna in 1930, giving pointers to youthful collectors, and he himself went off to the Burgenland region of Austria to record songs and tales in Yiddish dialect.

As a collector, Cahan perfectly understood the techniques now accepted as standard procedure in the field. He stressed the necessity of setting down texts faithfully, distinguishing between genuine and spurious traditions, establishing rapport with informants, preparing informal questionnaires in advance, steering the interview session with gentle leading questions, collecting what the informant had to offer and not what the collector desired.[4] Appreciating the wry Jewish jokelore, Cahan broadened the field of Jewish folktales from the Haggada to include secular and everyday themes.

Through the 1930's and 1940's, folklore research steadily developed in Palestine. One vein of interest, reaching back to J. E. Hanauer's 1907 collection, *Folk-Lore of the Holy Land,* emphasized the folk materials, Jewish and Arabic, long enduring in Palestine. A second approach stressed the study of isolated Jewish communities outside Palestine, such as Kurdistan and Yemen in the Middle East, whose folk customs had congealed in distinctive forms. The transference of the Jewish folklore movement from eastern Europe to Israel gave a new impetus and detachment to the study of Judeo-Slavic and Judeo-Germanic traditions. Combining all these interests, a Hebrew Society for Folklore and Ethnology was founded in 1942 and in 1948 began publishing the journal *Yeda-'Am.*

In Jewish folktale studies, the next step forward came with the application of international classificatory systems to Jewish traditional narrative. In 1954 Dov Neuman (now Noy), born in Poland, presented as his doctoral dissertation in folklore at Indiana University a "Motif-Index of Talmudic-Midrashic Literature," relying in good measure on Ginzberg's sources and notes given in Volumes V and VI of *The Legends of the Jews.* In his motif-index for the haggadic materials, Noy identified the inter-

---

[4] Richard Bauman, "Y. L. Cahan's Instructions on Collecting Folklore," *New York Folklore Quarterly,* XVIII (1962), 284–89.

national themes of folk literature systematized by his thesis director, Stith Thompson, in the first edition of the *Motif-Index of
Folk-Literature* (1932–36). When Thompson issued a greatly expanded edition of the *Motif-Index* (1955–58), he in turn incor-
porated Noy's motifs, thus placing the Jewish traditions in a
world-wide context. On his return to Israel late in 1954, Noy
initiated various folklore activities, teaching folklore at the Hebrew University in Jerusalem and organizing an Israel Folktale
Archives and Ethnological Museum at Haifa.

For a comparative folklorist, the diversity of cultural back-
grounds in Israel, united by a common religious and ethnic tradition, presented a unique and unparalleled field laboratory. Since
its establishment as an independent nation-state in 1948, the ingathering from Jewish communities in north Africa, the Middle
East, and eastern Europe has greatly accelerated. Immigrants had
been drifting into Palestine since 1882, the beginning of the
modern resettlement, when some 24,000 Jews lived in Palestine.
By 1948 the figure had grown to 650,000, of whom 452,000 had
entered as immigrants under the British rule commencing in
1919. In 1962 the total population reached upwards of 2,000,000,
of whom 172,000 were Moslems, 52,000 Christians, and 24,000
Druses. Of the Jewish population, 37 per cent were native-born,
35 per cent had come from Europe, America, and Oceania, 16
per cent from Asia, and 12 per cent from Africa. Some of the
Jewish communities in eastern Europe no longer existed, and only
their representatives in Israel could speak for their cultures.
Peoples from Moslem and Christian countries separated originally
by thousands of miles now lived as neighbors. As Noy has written,
"A pleasant walk separates Bokhara from Libya, Afghanistan
from Lithuania, Tunisia from Rumania." He planned systematic
collecting from all these groups.

Various agencies and individuals in three cities responded to
Noy's proposal for a folktale archives. Faculty members of Hebrew University in Jerusalem, municipal officers of Haifa, and
the editors of the Hebrew daily, *Omer,* published in Tel Aviv,
all co-operated to spread the net for raconteurs. From 1955 on, the
Omer carried a weekly column, "Mi-pi-ha-'am" ("From the Folk-
Mouth"), which printed some six hundred tales recorded in the

Israel Folktale Archives, along with information on the storyteller and his background. These stories attracted potential informants, who in turn contributed their texts to the collectors of
the Archives. Informants, who were never paid, appreciated the
opportunity to preserve the oral inheritance of their family, community, and country. The *Omer* catered particularly to the Olim,
or newcomers, printing its news and features in vocalized spell-
ing to assist readers whose Hebrew was still inadequate. Noy
had to convince intellectuals from the Middle East who were
zealously acquiring the Israeli culture that the humble folk literature of their original communities should be recognized as a
genuine contribution to the new synthetic heritage of Israel.

To train collectors and stimulate informants, Noy instituted
special means of instruction apart from regular university channels. An annual "Day of Study," sponsored by the Israel Section
for Folktale Research of the Yeda-Am (Jewish Folklore) Society,
provided him with the opportunity for informal discussion of
folktale collecting, archiving, and research methods. The meet-
ings were held in a settlement in the Judean hills called "The
Fields of Micha" in honor of Micha Josef Bin Gorion, the eminent author of *Der Born Judas*. (For this six-volume compendium
of Jewish religious and secular folk-narratives, issued from 1916 to
1923, Bin Gorion sifted a plethora of literary sources to cover all
manner of stories, from deeds of martyrs and holy men and famous prophets to magic tales and local legends.) During the Day
of Study, outstanding raconteurs related their tales to the research
groups, and prizes were awarded to collectors and storytellers
who had distinguished themselves in the past year. As a consequence of these activities, the materials in the Israel Folktale
Archives by the close of 1962 exceeded five thousand tales.

Six key indexes in the Archives, for Informants, Collectors,
Languages, Land of Origin, Heroes, and Tale Types, furnish information on the recorded tales.[5]

Among the informants of the first thousand tales gathered in
the Archives, one outdistanced all the rest, Yefet Shvili of Yemen,

---

[5] The data on the Archives in this Foreword was obtained from the
article by Noy, "The First Thousand Folktales in the Israel Folktale
Archives," in *Fabula*, IV (1961), 99–110.

a manual laborer, who contributed one hundred thirteen narratives. In second place came Mordechai "Marko" Litsi of Turkey with twenty-two. Collectors, who voluntarily contribute their services, are clerks, journalists, housewives, merchants, and residents of homes for the aged. Not all collectors are Jewish; a Druse student at Hebrew University, Salman Falah, has obtained tales from the Druse village of Sumie, and a Christian Arab who is a free-lance writer, Atallah Mantsour, has secured Arabic traditions in Galilee.

The unity of biblical folk-narratives in Jewish and Arab storytelling circles is readily evident in such collections as Hanauer's *Folk-Lore of the Holy Land: Moslem, Christian and Jewish* (1907) and Joseph Meyouhas' *Bible Tales in Arab Folk-Lore* (1928). In his Preface Meyouhas points out that the Syrian Arabs are descended directly from the Canaanites and Philistines, as the modern Jews are descended from the ancient Israelites, and hence the Arabs continue to tell their side of the story. "To the fellahin and bedawin, Noah was a skilful carpenter, Abraham a super-Sheik, Moses an inspired warrior, David an Emir, Isaiah an inscrutable man-of-Allah. . . ." The Koran contains many rabbinic and talmudic stories, which were often planted there by Christian sects living in the Middle East and inheriting the same legendary themes as did the authors of the Talmud and Midrash.[6]

The language index in the Archives indicates whether tongues other than Hebrew were used to record the tales. The principal languages are Yiddish, German, and English. Jewish collectors knowing no Arabic collected in English from Arabic informants knowing no Hebrew.

The index of lands or communities of origin reveals twenty-eight different countries or communities represented in the first thousand IFA entries. The highest scoring areas are Yemen, eastern Europe, Palestine, Iraq, Turkey, and Tunisia.

Under the index "Heroes," the archivists list biblical or historical personalities around whom narratives center. Of ninety-four such heroes, the prophet Elijah has attracted the most legends. The miracles and prophecies of Solomon, David, and Moses also

[6] Haim Schwarzbaum, "The Jewish and Moslem Versions of Some Theodicy Legends," *Fabula*, III (1960), 119–69.

win considerable attention. No less favored are Maimonides, the twelfth-century Jewish sage, Rabbi Shalom Shabazi, an illustrious Yemenite poet, and the Baal-Shem Tov, celebrated founder of the eighteenth-century hasidic movement. Among modern heroes, Rothschild is the favorite Jewish personality and Napoleon the favorite non-Jewish one. Moslem and Christian heroes, such as Harun Al-Rashid, Mohammed, and Jesus, are remembered in Israel.

Finally, the index of tale types identifies a given narrative according to the standard international systems.

From this exciting and unique archives are drawn the tales of faith and magic and wit that appear on the following pages.

RICHARD M. DORSON

Introduction

Since Biblical times, narration has been regarded as an art among the Jewish people. During the postbiblical period, literature was transmitted orally and the official name given to this era of Hebrew literature is "Torah Sheb'al Peh," which means Oral Law. In the rich Talmudic-Midrashic literature, one can still observe signs of oral transmission.

The various communities of Israel cultivated the art of storytelling during the years of their long dispersion. The social institution of the sermon (*derasha*) was the most popular attraction within the Jewish communities of East and West, and the preacher (*darshan*) was the main instrument of diffusion.

In addition to this religious channel—for the sermon took place at the synagogue and was strongly influenced by religious ideas —there were also secular channels of transmission. The synagogue sermon has never replaced these evenings of storytelling. Unfortunately, modern Jewish authors and scholars have focused their attention mainly on religious tales, which were published in collections from the beginning of Jewish printing and thus attracted the attention of Jewish scholars. However, the secular current continued to flow in its own way even if the flow was often underground. Only thirty years ago, the distinguished Jewish folklorist, Y. L. Cahan, drew the attention of Jewish scholars and folklorists to the rich secular lore of the east European Jews. Owing to the energetic work done by the collectors and scholars of the Yiddish Scientific Institution (Yivo) in Vilna, Poland, and after World War II in New York, the secular folktales transmitted by the Jews of eastern Europe in Yiddish are now well known.

Unluckily, no Cahan arose among the Oriental Jews, and only after the establishment of the state of Israel, and the "ingathering of the exiled communities" in their new homeland, did it become evident that our notion about the character of the Jewish Oriental folktale was also false. Of course, the religious story, with its ethical background and its concluding moral, is still conspicuous in the literary treasury of the Jewish-Oriental communities, but it is far from being dominant.

The folktales collected under my supervision in the state of Israel since 1955 from narrators originating in over thirty Jewish communities bear witness to the fact that the magic and secular folktale still plays an important role in the life, imagination, and creation of these people. From among over two thousand six hundred stories collected by the Israel Section for Folktale Research and preserved at the Israel Ethnological Museum and Folklore Archives (Haifa), a sample of seventy-one stories has been chosen that is a true reflection of the material in general. The wide dispersion of the narrators, who originate from East and West, testifies that the Jewish narrator still carries and spreads tale types and tale motifs from one cultural area to another.

The notes to each story are not meant to give a complete scholarly background with all the known versions and parallels. They indicate the serial number of the story in the IFA (Israel Folktale Archives), the name and the place of origin of the narrator, and the most important data that help to clarify the main type and motifs of the story. The Type- and Motif-Index tables at the end of the collection are meant for the scholar interested in comparative research on the stories published. The glossary will enable the non-Jewish reader to understand expressions of a local and linguistic nature.

In the notes, emphasis has been placed on parallel versions in the cultural area where the storyteller heard his tale. Special attention is given to recent Soviet collections from Asia, generally unknown to the Western scholar. These cover oral material from central Asia and from the Caucasus, which is affiliated with the oral literature of Turkey, Persia, Afghanistan, India, and Arabia and, therefore, with their Jewish populations. Closer examination of these ties will reward students of the folktale.

As head of the Israel Section for Folktale Research and director of IFA, I should like to express thanks to the translator of the original Hebrew text into English, Mrs. Gene Baharav, and to the two secretaries of the Section, Miss Elisheva Schoenfeld (1955–58) and Mrs. Heda Jason (1958–61), who helped to collect many of the stories, to arrange them in the Archives, and to index them. The Hebrew University in Jerusalem placed at my disposal a five-year Warburg Fellowship, which freed me in part from my teaching duties and allowed me to devote time to organizing the net of volunteer and trained collectors. I should also like to thank Professors E. E. Urbach, head of the Hebrew University Institute for Jewish Studies, Shimeon Halkin, chairman of the Department for Hebrew Literature, and Dov Sadan, chairman of the Department of Yiddish Literature. The Haifa Municipality endorsed the plan to establish in that city the first Ethnological Museum in Israel, in which the IFA collection is housed, and its mayor, Abba Khoushi, has always shown much interest in and understanding of the Museum's scholarly goals. The late editor of the Tel Aviv daily *Omer* and chairman of the Israel Association of Journalists, Dan Pines, and his successor, Dr. Zvi Rotem, have helpfully opened their columns to the publication of IFA folktales.

My former student, Dan Ben-Amos, now a graduate student at Indiana University, has greatly aided in the preparation of the manuscript. Much of the correspondence and matters of detail were handled by Heda Jason. Richard M. Dorson, the series editor, encouraged me in this undertaking and has helped overcome the difficulties caused by distance.

But my main gratitude goes to the dozens of collectors and narrators who did their best to preserve the tales for the wide public in Israel and abroad as well as for future generations. Thanks to them and their ancient tales, the motifs common to all the Jewish communities become clearer, and their origin is clarified.

In Israel a new synthetic culture is being created out of diverse traditions. Let us hope that the collection and preservation of oral Jewish folktales will lead to a genuine Hebrew folk literature based on ancient traditions and characteristics of the entire Jewish people. We hope that this modest collection will bring that character to the knowledge of readers and scholars all over the world, especially to those who do not know the Hebrew language.

Dov Noy

Hebrew University, Jerusalem

Contents

III. TALKING ANIMALS

IV. KINGS AND COMMONERS

V. CLEVER JEWS

VI. HUSBANDS AND WIVES

VII. HEROES AND HEROINES

VIII. WISE MEN

IX. NUMSKULLS

Part I
The Righteous

· 1 · The Wayfarer and His Ass

IFA 1183. Recorded by Zvulun Kort, as heard in his youth in Afghanistan.

Another version of this text, from Palestine, is given in J. E. Hanauer, The Folk-Lore of the Holy Land, *pp. 234–37, and one from central Asia is given in W. Sidelnikov,* Kazakh Folktales, *No. 24. This form of the tale of the "pious animal" (cf. Type 1842,* The Testament of the Dog) *is widespread in the Moslem cultural area in connection with the worship of graves of holy men. See R. Kriss and H. Kriss-Heinrich,* Volksglaube im Bereich das Islam, *Vol. I:* Wallfahrtswesen und Heiligenverehrung *(Wiesbaden, 1960).*

· A MOSLEM WAYFARER had an ass. This ass was his only possession, and therefore he loved him more than anything else. On his wanderings the ass died, and the Moslem went about sad and depressed. One day he reached a village, whose sheik, taking pity on him, gave him a fine young foal. The wayfarer loved the ass as it was a support and help to him on his wanderings.

One day the ass dropped down and died. The wayfarer dug him a grave and put up two poles on the hillock. He fixed up a cloth as a banner to indicate that his long-eared friend was buried there. Then he sat on the hillock and mourned for seven days. On the seventh day a passer-by saw our friend sitting on the hillock with tears flowing from his eyes like water. Thought the man, "Truly, a holy one must be buried here." He took out a coin from his pocket and handed it to the wayfarer. More people went by that day, and one by one they handed coins to the wayfarer. The coming day more people passed by, and some of them remained on the hillock, built dwelling places, and put up a minaret.

Word spread through the land that a holy man was buried in this place, and people came from all corners of the country and gave their offerings in money, livestock, and possessions. Even those ravished by disease came to seek a cure. It became known that the wayfarer was a benevolent man, and he extended his mercy to all seeking justice.

Word reached the sheik, the very one who had given the foal to the wanderer, and he came to pray. He ascended the minaret and then lay on the grave of the holy one on the hillock. But how amazed he was when he saw there the unfortunate wayfarer. They were very pleased to meet each other. The sheik asked, "Tell me, my friend, what is the name of the holy man buried here?"

The eyes of the wayfarer darkened with embarrassment, and he began stammering," I . . . I . . . I will tell you the truth itself. No holy one but the ass you gave me is buried in the hillock. It died, and I buried it here."

The sheik burst out laughing. "Do you remember the grave of the holy one at my village and the minaret there?"

"Of course, I remember, I remember."

"If so, my dear friend," the sheik consoled him, "do not worry. No holy one is buried there, but the mother of the ass that you buried here."

• 2 • *The Two She-Goats from Shebreshin*

IFA 532. Narrated to Dov Noy by an elderly Polish Jew.

On underground caves and passages (Motif F721.1) leading from the Lands of Dispersion to the Land of Israel, see Dov Noy, The Diaspora and the Land of Israel (Hebrew), p. 44; Yiddisher Folklor (1938), ed. Y. L. Cahan, No. 20, p. 147; and the short story of the famous Hebrew novelist Sh. Y. Agnon (b. 1888), "A Story with a She-Goat," in Collected Stories of Sh. Y. Agnon, II: These and These (Tel Aviv, 1959), 373–75 (Hebrew). The she-goat also plays an important role in the legends of the journey of Rabbi Israel Baal Shem Tov to the Holy Land. Shebreshin was one of the nine Polish villages settled by Jews expelled from Spain. The folk etymology explains the origin of the name of the village from the Hebrew "Shev Rishon" (Sit first!); see Cahan (1938), No. 23, p. 148. Relevant motifs are D2131, "Magic underground journey," D1555, "Underground passage magically opens," F92, "Pit entrance to lower world," F111, "Journey to earthly paradise," F721.1, "Underground passages. Journey made through natural subways," B103.0.5, "Treasure-producing goat," B563.4, "Animal leads cleric to holy place," and N773, "Adventure from following animal to cave (lower world)."

• IN THE WOODS near the Polish village of Shebreshin, there once lived a poor Hasid with his wife. Every Sabbath the Hasid used to go to the village to pray and study in the synagogue. And what did he do the rest of the week? No one knows. Only this is known: he had two she-goats that gave but little milk. Every day the Hasid's wife would let the goats loose in the field, and in the evening she would tie them up. The Hasid and his wife used to sell goat's milk, butter, and cheese, but they earned very little.

One day the woman went to milk the goats, but they were not there. The Hasid and his wife searched for them in the woods but did not find them. The wife remembered that in the morning she had forgotten to tether them. She began to cry and to shout, but her husband stopped her, saying with a smile on his lips, "Everything is from Heaven."

The woman looked into her husband's eyes and understood that there was something mysterious in the matter. She recalled how her husband had longed to buy the goats and to rear them. He had said then, "It is the will of Heaven."

At sunset the goats came home again and that same evening they gave a great deal of milk—more than any other time. The Hasid's wife took this as a sign that the goats had been blessed. And on the following day she did not tether them again.

Once more she could not find the goats during the daytime, but in the evening they returned, heavy with milk. The Hasid and his wife sold the milk in the village, and lo! it was unlike any other milk. This milk restored the health of the sick, and even those who were very ill became well after drinking it. Soon there were no more sick people in the whole village of Shebreshin.

Six days passed. On the seventh day the Hasid decided to follow the goats into the woods. The goats scampered along, and he went after them. They came to a place where the trees were close upon each other, tree upon tree. The goats darted under the trees. The Hasid went after them. There was an opening in the ground near these trees, and the goats went through it. The Hasid followed them. Suddenly he found himself inside a cave and saw from afar a beam of light. The goats scrambled toward the light. The Hasid followed them.

On the way jumping black devils with tongues of red flames appeared. They shouted until they rent the skies. Stones fell from all sides. The sound of silver coins jingled behind him, and naked women appeared near him. But the Hasid went on and on. He did not look to the right, and he did not look to the left. His faith in Heaven did not leave him, not for a second. And so the evil forces who were disturbing him left him, one by one. The Hasid reached the light at the opening of the cave. Climbing out, he saw the blue sky and a young boy standing and piping a tune to his goats. Seeing the Hasid, the youth approached him and asked in Hebrew, "Are you new in our district?"

The Hasid stood in awe because he realized that his feet were on the holy soil of the Land of Israel. The youth continued to speak, "I am also new here in the surroundings of Safed. Until now I used to take my goats to the Judean Hills, to the mountains of the Holy City of Jerusalem."

The Hasid threw himself on the ground, kissed the soil and the stones, and gave thanks to the Lord. Then he sat down and wrote a letter to the Jews of Shebreshin and to all the Jews in the galuth. He called upon them to come and not to be frightened by the things they saw in the cave, which were phantoms without reality. The Hasid put the letter in a big fig leaf, tied it to the neck of one of the goats, and wrote on the fig leaf that the letter should be handed to the rabbi of Shebreshin.

That same evening the goats returned home, heavy with milk. The Hasid's wife saw that her husband had not come back and was very upset. In fact, she was so worried that she did not notice the fig leaf tied round the goat's neck.

The woman waited one day, two days, three days, and her husband still did not come. She was sure that robbers in the woods had killed him, and she asked herself why she should remain in

the woods? It would be better to move to the village of Shebreshin
and live within the Jewish community! So she said, and so she
did. And what does one need goats for in the village? It would be
better to have them slaughtered and sell the meat. So she said, and
so she did.

Only after slaughtering the goats did the shohet find the letter
in the fig leaf, and he immediately called the rabbi. When the
rabbi had read the letter, he began weeping, "What can be done
now? The goats cannot be returned to life, and only they know
the way to the Holy Land."

The rabbi decided that the Jews of Shebreshin should neither
eat nor drink for three days; they should pray. Probably because
of their bad deeds, the letter had not been found in time, and
they would not be able to reach the Holy Land. Now they had to
go on waiting in the galuth for redemption.

The rabbi of Shebreshin kept the letter for many years in the
synagogue. When the great fire came and most of Shebreshin
went up in flame, the letter from the Holy Land was lost too.

•3• *King David's Tomb in Jerusalem*

*IFA 966. Recorded by Nehama Zion from Miriam Tschernobilski,
born in Poland.*

*The tale centers around Motifs D1960.2, "Kyffhäuser: king
asleep in mountain," and C897.3, "Tabu: calculating time of Messiah's advent." Jewish folklore is filled with stories of how pious
rabbis attempted, and failed, to bring the Messiah down to earth.
The relationship between Elijah and the Messiah is discussed by
E. Margolioth in* Elijah the Prophet in Jewish Literature *(Hebrew), pp. 156–77. In Jewish tradition the true Messiah is a descendant of King David, whereas the false one is related to the
house of Joseph. Other tales connected with King David's tomb
are found in J. E. Hanauer,* The Folk-Lore of the Holy Land, *pp.
89–93, 132–33. Another version of the present text is in A. Ben-
Israel Avi-Oded,* Legends of the Land of Israel *(Hebrew), pp.
220–21.*

• EIGHTY YEARS AGO, in a Polish yeshiva, there were two pupils who were aroused with a longing for redemption. Both of them eagerly desired to ascend to Eretz Yisrael, the Land of the Fathers. They especially wished to see King David's tomb. Day and night they dreamed about it, and at last they began to think how to turn their dreams into reality. They did not have money, so they decided to ascend on foot. As they decided, so they did. They set off taking only sticks and knapsacks. On the way they met with many obstacles, but with the help of God they overcame them all and arrived at last at the holy city of Jerusalem. They trembled and were happy in their hearts to be at the holy place and to arrive safe and sound at their destination. Still overcome with joy, they found themselves suddenly just opposite the walls of Mt. Zion. They did not know, however, exactly where King David's tomb was or which road led there. While they were wondering, Elijah the Prophet, of blessed memory, appeared before them and showed them the way.

"Now my sons, when you reach the tomb and when you enter and go down the steps, keep to the bottom of the tomb. Your eyes will be blinded by all the visions of desire that you see there, silver, gold, and diamonds. Woe if you should lose your senses! You must look for the jug of water at King David's head. Pour water from the jug onto King David's hands as he stretches them toward you. Pour water three times over each hand, and then the King will rise up and we shall be redeemed. For King David is not dead; he lives and exists. He is dreaming, and he will arise when we are worthy of it. By your virtue and the merit of your longing and love, he will arise and redeem. Amen, that this may come to pass."

As Elijah the Prophet finished these words, he disappeared. The young men then ascended Mt. Zion, guarded by Elijah, the Prophet. They went down into the depth of King David's tomb. Just as Elijah the Prophet had said, so it was. King David stretched out his hands to them, and there was a jug of water at his head. But because of our many sins, the riches around blinded the young men's eyes, and they forgot to pour water onto the hands outstretched toward them. In anguish the hands fell back and immediately the King's image disappeared.

The young men were startled when they realized that through

them the redemption had been delayed again and the galuth would go on longer. They both wept from bitter anguish because the mitzvah of redemption had been in their hands and they had let it slip through their fingers.

May it come to pass that silver and gold will no longer dazzle our eyes. And when the right hour comes again, let it not be delayed. Amen and Amen.

·4· Joseph the Righteous of Peki'in

IFA 437. Recorded by Min'am Haddad, an Arab teacher from Peki'in, as heard from A. Zinati, a Sephardic Jew born in that Arab village.

The tenth man required for a minyan is a common motif in Jewish folklore and a subject of both jokes and religious legends. In many tales Elijah the Prophet completes the minyan, e.g., see J. E. Hanauer, The Folk-Lore of the Holy Land, pp. 57–58. For references to this motif in Jewish humorous tales, see R. M. Dorson, "Jewish-American Dialect Stories on Tape," in R. Patai, F. L. Utley, and D. Noy (eds.), Studies in Biblical and Jewish Folklore, No. 61, p. 158, and headnotes thereto. A recent American literary treatment is The Tenth Man, by Paddy Chayefsky (New York, 1959). Another version of our tale is found in M. Ben-Yehezkel, The Book of Tales (Hebrew), V, 367–71. Motifs D1472.1.22, "Magic bag (sack) supplies food," and D1652.5.11, "Inexhaustible meal sack," have a Biblical parallel; see I Kings 17:14. Motifs C423.1, "Tabu: disclosing source of magic power," F348.5.1.1, "Mortal not to tell secret of gift of inexhaustible meat," and the general Motif Q 140, "Miraculous or magic rewards," are present.

• HUNDREDS OF YEARS AGO, when the village of Peki'in in Galilee was entirely Jewish, there lived a man named Joseph, who was pious and kindhearted. He followed the path of God and heeded his bidding. The man and his wife earned their living tilling their land, like all the other inhabitants of the village.

There was no mill in Peki'in, so whoever wanted to grind grain had to go to the Casib wadi, whose source is at the foot of the Meron Mountains and which flows into the Mediterranean near Gesher Haziv. There was plenty of water in the river, quite enough to move the mills.

Every month Joseph used to go to that spot after his wife had cleaned and washed the grain in order to grind it at the mill. Once on his way home from the mill, he passed through a wadi, west of the village of Peki'in. He began to hum a tune that he had learned from his father, blessed be his memory, who had been the chief cobbler of Peki'in. At last Joseph reached the spring Ein Tiria at the foot of the mountain, not far from the bottom of the wadi. There, at the tomb of the famous sage Abba Hoshaya, he sat down to quench his thirst and to rest from his long journey. Before he had reached the main road again, he heard a voice from the foot of the mountain. He looked up and saw a group of men in black standing there, beckoning to him.

Then an old man with a long white beard approached him and called out, "We are nine rabbis here. We want to pray and we need a tenth to complete the minyan. Come and pray with us, if you are a Jew."

Joseph tied his donkey to the tree and followed in the footsteps of the old man along the slope of the mountain.

When the prayer was over and Joseph was ready to leave, the old rabbi said to him, "Take these three pebbles, and put them into your sack of flour. It will never empty as long as you keep the secret in your heart. But you must know that once you reveal this to anybody, your wife and all your family will die." The old man finished his words, and put three pebbles in Joseph's hand.

Joseph put the pebbles into his sack and rode off on his donkey. One month passed, then two and three went by. Every time his wife took flour to knead dough, she found the sack still full. She was very curious to know the reason. Her husband, however, did not want to reveal it to her and said, "We neither quarrel between ourselves nor work on holidays and Saturdays, so God has granted us his blessings." His wife was not satisfied with such a meaningless explanation and said, "I shall leave you forever if you do not disclose the secret."

At last Joseph gave in to her and told her about the prayer and the minyan.

That night the old man appeared to Joseph and said to him, "Because you are righteous, your wife and children will not die, but your sack will become empty and you will never again live in peace and contentment. From this day on you will be in discord with your wife."

Joseph broke out into tears and pleaded, but to no avail. As the old one had said, so it was. From that day on Joseph began to quarrel with his wife, and his life was filled with sorrow.

Years passed, and Joseph died and was buried in his garden. The miracle that had happened to him became known to people of the village, and they added "the righteous" to his name. Until this very day you can see in Peki'in the "Garden of Joseph the Righteous," but most people believe that it was named after Joseph, son of Jacob the Patriarch.

· 5 · *The Rich Miser and the Shoemaker*

IFA 271. Recorded by Tsipora Rabin, housewife, in Tel Aviv from Rabbi Bernstein, born in Russia.

The secret righteous who excel in charity are very common in Jewish folklore of the East and the West. Cf. Motifs V433, "Charity of saints," and Q44.2, "Man pardoned for short accounts when it is learned that he has given money to the poor as alms."

· IN A CERTAIN village there lived a rich Jew. He was a miser and never gave alms to the poor. Once a man came and asked for alms. The rich man asked, "Where do you come from?"

"Here from the village," answered the beggar.

"It is impossible!" exclaimed the rich man. "Here everybody knows that I do not give alms."

In the same town there lived another Jew, a shoemaker. He was a great benefactor, and with open hands he gave alms to everyone that turned to him.

One day the rich man died. The Jews of the village, and the

rabbi, the head of their community, decided to bury the rich
miser near the fence. They did not even follow the funeral procession to the cemetery.

Several days passed. When the poor beggars came, as usual, to
the shoemaker to beg for alms, he answered, "I have nothing to
give you."

"How is it possible? What has happened?" wondered the
people.

The shoemaker was called to the rabbi's house and asked,
"How is it that a man like you has stopped distributing alms?"

The shoemaker related the following story: "Many years ago
the rich man who passed away a few days ago came to me with a
great sum of money for distribution to charity, on condition that
I would not disclose to anyone where the money came from. And
so it was. I promised him I would not reveal his secret until the
day of his death. He used to give me all the money and I used to
be the so-called benefactor. Now, with the death of the rich man,
I have not a farthing to give, because I myself am a poor man."

When the rabbi heard the story, he called all the villagers together, and they went to the grave of the "wicked one" and
begged his forgiveness for the evil and humiliation that they had
caused him. In his will the rabbi asked that he be buried near
the fence, next to the grave of the rich man.

•6• *He Who Has Faith in God Is Rewarded*

IFA 1627. Recorded by Hanina Mizrahi, as heard in his youth in Iran.

A variant is given in M. Gaster, The Exempla of the Rabbis,
*No. 414, pp. 159–60, 262. Among his references Gaster cites such
well-known literary collections as Boccaccio,* Decameron, *10th
day, 1st tale;* Gesta Romanorum, *No. 109; Benfey,* Pantschatantra,
I, 604; and Bin Gorion, Der Born Judas, *II, 260, 356. Motifs pres-*

ent are Q4, "Humble rewarded, haughty punished"; Q22, "Reward for faith"; and Q221.6, "Lack of trust in God punished."

• A RICH MAN put aside a hundred *toman* (Persian money) for a poor man smitten by fate who through bitterness in his soul had ceased to have faith in God.

The rich man put the hundred *toman* in his girdle and went to the market. Idlers were lounging around, and the rich man approached them saying, "He who will announce before the crowd that he has no longer faith in God will receive a hundred *toman* from me." He took out a bundle and raised it before the eyes of the beggars. They called out to him with contempt, "Away! Go away from here! Our eyes are always turned to the mercy of God, and we shall rely on him till our last day."

The rich man left the beggars and went to a deserted place where he found a naked man lying upon ashes. The rich man said to him, "Get up, you miserable beaten creature. Take this bundle of a hundred *toman,* so as to revive your starving soul, and confess that you no longer have faith in the Lord Almighty."

"No, no!" said the naked one. "Till my last breath I shall not stop relying on the help of God."

"Alas!" sighed the rich man. "I have not found among the living a single man who does not have faith in God. I shall hand over my money to the dead, who no doubt have lost all hope."

The rich man went to the cemetery, dug a pit at one of the tombstones, and called: "Awake, awake, you eternal dead, who have lost all hope, and take my money for yourself." Then he went home.

Years passed. The wheel of fortune turned for the rich man. He lost all his wealth and had to live on dry bread and water. In the bitterness of his soul, he went to the cemetery where he had hidden his money. He hoped that by finding it he would be able to keep himself and his family from starving.

As he was digging, the cemetery guards caught him and reported to the police that time and again he had been stealing winding sheets off the dead and that he had a bundle of money that surely came from one of the graves.

The police found the bundle of money on the man and thrust him in prison without heeding his words.

The next day he was brought before the king for judgment. The prisoner confessed and said, "I sinned against the Almighty and hid my money in graves of the dead, who, I believed, had lost all hope. Through stupidity I became poor and went to the cemetery to dig out the bundle of money I hid there years ago. The cemetery guards caught me, bringing a false charge against me. Merciful king, have pity on me."

The king recognized him saying, "Do you not know that the help of God comes in the twinkling of an eye? I am that naked man you once found on the ashes, and with the help of the Almighty, I ascended to the throne. He who has faith in God is rewarded."

And he gave orders to the police, "Return the bundle of money to this poor man, and let him go. His words hold true."

· 7 ·   *The Drought in Mosul*

IFA 719. Recorded by Moshe Wigiser in Herzliya in 1955 from Moshe Morad, born in Mosul, Iraq.

In many Oriental countries Arabs regard Jews as rain makers and hence think of drought as caused by unwillingness of the Jews to pray for rain. In many tales the Arab king threatens his Jewish citizens with death or expulsion if the drought continues. For discussion and references, see Dov Noy on "Rain Folklore," in Encyclopaedia Hebraica, *s.v. "Geshem" (Rain). The Persian idea that the Jews are especially learned in rain making is evident in a fourth-century Babylonian talmudical story (Taanit 24b) about King Shapur, his mother, and the sage Rava.*

Cf. Dov Noy, "Simpleton's Prayer Brings Down Rain" (Hebrew), a discussion of Type 827, A Shepherd Knows Nothing of God, and Motifs D2143.1.3, "Rain produced by prayer," and V51.1, "Man who does not know how to pray so holy that he walks on water," in Machnayim, *No. 51 (1960), 34–45, esp. p. 39.*

• IN THE TOWN of Mosul in northern Babylon (Iraq), the Jews and Moslems lived side by side for many generations in peace and mutual understanding. But in the old times the devil was always playing mischief between them, and quarrels broke out very frequently.

It came to pass one year that no rain fell in the country, and the sky ceased to drench the earth. The Feast of Hanukkah passed by, and still no rain fell. Then came the fifteenth of Shebat, the Festival of Trees, and still there was no rain. The people began to clasp their hands in anguish, saying: "Woe to us! The year will be a year of drought. Woe to us!"

In the meantime food became expensive, and the price of wheat kept going up from week to week.

On Friday, the Moslem day of prayer, all the Moslems went to the great Mosque of Mosul and prayed. But all in vain.

When the Moslems saw that their prayers were not being answered, their sorrow increased. They approached their Jewish neighbors and pleaded, "Forgive us our quarrels in the past, and you too call upon your God. Maybe he will listen to you and send rain to the parched earth. Then we will be rescued, thanks to you, and we shall not die."

All the Jews of Mosul, both young and old, gathered together in the synagogue, and from there they went to the old cemetery of their forefathers and rabbis, who had been wise and holy men. The Jews prayed in a loud voice and cried bitterly, "Rescue us, our Lord, and give rain to our lands. Why must we and our children die, together with our Moslem neighbors?"

And while they went on praying and wailing, the sky became covered with heavy black clouds, and rain began to pour down on the earth.

When the Moslems saw this, they hurried to the Jewish cemetery, raised the Jews on their shoulders, and amid music and dancing, they carried them to their homes.

And from that time on, there was only peace and love between the Jews of Mosul and their Moslem neighbors.

.8. The Town That Had Faith in God

IFA 186. Recorded by David Alkayam from Rafael Uhna, born in Morocco.

This text combines Types 1199, The Lord's Prayer, *and 332IV episode (a),* Death Avenges Self by Tricking the Man into Finishing the Prayer, *and contains Motifs C785, "Tabu: trying to save provision for another day," Q221.6, "Lack of trust in God punished," and G303.3.1.12, "The devil as a well-dressed gentleman." The first cultural hero in Jewish tradition who tried to prolong his life by studying holy scripts when he was about to die was King David. See L. Ginzberg,* The Legends of the Jews, *IV, 113–14, VI, 271.*

• THIS IS A story of a town whose inhabitants were pious and had faith in God. Not one of them used to save, not even a penny, because they said, "We must eat and drink today, and as for tomorrow, we will trust in God." Therefore there was not a rich man among them.

One of the inhabitants, named Meir, was a watchman. He carried out his work diligently and wholeheartedly. But he had an evil wife, and she did not trust in God. Day and night she used to nag her husband, "Let us save money for our old age." But Meir always answered, "I trust in God, so we should not be afraid."

The woman was barren, and since they had no children, she was very concerned about their old age. "Who will sustain us tomorrow?"

"Confidence in God's power is a great thing," her husband used to say. "So do not fear."

The Almighty, blessed be he, looked on and said to the Angel of Death, "Go and fetch the soul of Meir from the town of my faithful ones, because he no longer trusts in me."

When Meir returned from work, the Angel of Death awaited

him, disguised as a porter and carrying two sacks of flour. He
said to Meir, "A rich man sent me with flour for the inhabitants
of this town; so you distribute it, but forego your own portion."

Meir did as he was bidden. He went from house to house with
the flour. However, the inhabitants refused to accept it saying,
"Today we have food, and as for tomorrow, we trust in God."

Meir returned to the porter and related all that had happened.
The porter disclosed the truth: that he was the Angel of Death
and had come to take away Meir's soul because he no longer had
faith in God. Meir pleaded with the angel, "Promise not to take
away my soul until I have prayed the *Shema* prayer: 'Hear, O
Israel.'"

The Angel of Death agreed and said, "I shall be damned if I
take your soul before you have prayed the 'Hear, O Israel.'"

Meir began the prayer but interrupted it and said, "I shall be
damned if I ever complete this prayer." The angel realized that
Meir had deceived him; whereupon he disappeared.

Meir related to his wife everything that had happened. She
said, "Come, let us escape from the Angel of Death to another
town." And so they did.

After some time the Angel of Death disguised himself as a rich
man. He went to the same town and asked if he could be a guest
in Meir's home. The town notables informed him, "This Jew,
Meir, is a poor fellow. There are many benevolent and rich people who would like to entertain you. Would you not prefer their
hospitality?"

However, the guest would agree to stay with no one else but
Meir. The couple was very pleased with the guest, who did not
spare money on their account.

Whenever Meir prayed, the rich man listened to him. He noticed that every time Meir reached the prayer "Hear, O Israel,"
he used to skip the end, and never once did he complete it. So it
went on day by day.

One morning Meir's wife entered the rich man's room to
awaken him, as was her daily custom. Imagine her shock when
she saw that he was dying. Hastily she went to call her husband,
"Come quickly to recite 'Hear, O Israel' over the dying man.
Then we shall bury our guest in secret, and all his wealth will re-

main with us." At first Meir refused to fulfill his wife's request, but at last he gave in to her pleading and nagging.

Meir finished the *Shema* prayer, and the Angel of Death jumped out of the bed and seized his soul.

•9• *The Blessings of a Hidden Saint*

IFA 1828. Recorded by Nehama Zion from a Bessarabian woman.

The "simpleton's prayer" and the "secret righteous" are both common themes in Jewish folktales and are here combined in the final episode of the water-carrier's disappearance. Cf. the articles by Dov Noy in Machnayim: *"Simpleton's Prayer Brings Down Rain," No. 51 (1960), and "Men of Miracles in Jewish Folktales" (Hebrew), No. 63 (1961).*

• IN A CERTAIN village in Poland, there was a family of two, a husband and wife. They did not have children although they had been married for ten years. The man accepted his fate, for who is a man to question the ways of the Lord? The wife, however, would not resign herself to being barren, and she fought against her bad fortune, for of what value is wealth if one is without the most precious treasure of all, a child? She went from doctor to doctor and from specialist to specialist, but God did not make her fruitful. When she saw that the doctors and specialists could do nothing for her, she turned to saddiks, but they could not help her either. Still the woman would not give up hope. One day, she heard of a rabbi, a great miracle-maker, living in Warsaw, the capital. The long distance between her village and the capital did not dishearten her, and one day she set off to see the rabbi. He received her well, and she poured out her soul to him. She wept and pleaded, "Rabbi, bless me that I may have a son, or my life will not be worth living."

The rabbi listened to the woman and then asked her, "Where are you from?"

When he heard her answer, he smiled and said, "My good

woman, in your village lives a great saddik. Ask him to bless you. If he does so, the Lord will surely remember you, and you will have sons."

"Who is the great saddik?" asked the woman in astonishment. She knew everyone in the village, but had never heard of a saddik living there.

The rabbi asked, "Is there a water-drawer in the village?"

"Yes," she answered. "They say he is mad, and he lives with his mother in a tumble-down hut."

"That is the one," declared the rabbi. "Go home and ask him to bless you, and do not leave him until he has done so."

The woman could not believe her ears, but before she had time to say a word, the rabbi rose from his seat and the talk was over.

As the rabbi had bidden her, the woman went home, and early the following morning she set out to look for the "mad" water-drawer. She went to the village well, knowing that she would certainly find him there drawing water for the villagers. And indeed she saw him at the well, bent down under the weight of two water pitchers hanging from a stick across his back.

The woman did not hesitate for a moment. She hurriedly approached him and pleaded, "Bless me that I may have a child, a son."

On hearing her, the "madman" turned to her in astonishment and asked, "Who am I and what am I that you ask this from me? Am I not a simple water-carrier?"

"You have to bless me," pleaded the woman again and again. "I shall not let you go until you have blessed me." She burst out into a heartbreaking cry.

The "madman" turned to her and said, "What is to be done? Let me go, woman. You will have children, you will have children." So saying, he disappeared.

Since that time, no one saw the water-drawer any more, and no one knew his whereabouts. His mother and the tumble-down house also disappeared. It was the talk of the whole village, and no one understood why or how it had happened.

And the Lord remembered the woman and made her fruitful. Exactly one year after she had been blessed by the "madman," to her and her husband's joy, she gave birth to two sons. Of course, the entire village was proud and delighted. There was no limit to the happiness at their home, and their sons were brought up in the light of the Torah, mitzvoth, and good deeds.

·10· *When the Wheel of Fortune Turns*

IFA 541. Recorded by S. Gabai from Djudja Shaul, born in Iraq.

A version of Type 947A, Bad Luck Cannot Be Arrested, which has been reported from southeastern Europe. The hero of the present tale, Abraham Ibn-Ezra (1092–1176), was a poet and a scholar versatile in grammar, the Bible, philosophy, mathematics, and astronomy. He was born in Toledo, Spain, and left his country in 1140. In his wanderings he passed through Italy and France, arriving in London in 1158. His relationship with Maimonides (1135–1204), who lived most of his life in North Africa and Egypt, has not been documented. Ibn-Ezra could benefit neither from his immense knowledge nor from his poetic skill and lived in poverty all his life. He wrote about his misery in many poems, the most famous of which are self-descriptive, cynical epigrams:

Out of Luck

'Twas sure a luckless planet
That ruled when I was born—
I hoped for fame and fortune,
I have but loss and scorn.

An evil fate pursues me
With unrelenting spite,
If I sold lamps and candles
The sun would shine all night.

I cannot, cannot prosper,
No matter what I try—
Were selling shrouds my business,
No man would ever die!

[*Trans. S. Solis-Cohen, in* When Love Passed By and Other Verses (*Philadelphia, 1929*).]

Born without a Star

I come in the morn
To the house of the nobly born.
They say he rode away.
I come again at the end of the day,
But he is not at his best, and needs a rest.
He is either sleeping or riding afar—
Woe to the man who was born without a star.

[*Trans. Meyer Waxman, in* A History of Jewish Literature, *I* (*2d ed.; New York, 1938*), *p. 234.*]

On Abraham Ibn-Ezra, see A. E. Milgram, An Anthology of Medieval Hebrew Literature (*Philadelphia, 1935*), *pp. 67 ff., and J. H. Shirman,* Hebrew Poetry in Spain and Provence (*Hebrew*) (*2d ed.; Jerusalem-Tel Aviv, 1961*), *p. 575.*

• RABBI ABRAHAM IBN-EZRA lost his father, and his mother had to work very hard to provide for him and his younger brother. He studied the Torah at the house of learning, and being clever and very diligent, he grew up to be a great, wise rabbi. He used to help the needy although he had no money for himself. Week after week in his sermons he used to preach about the importance of charity. He always divided all the money collected among the poor. Yet he himself was very badly off, and luck was never with him, not even once. Whatever he turned to was a failure.

Rabbi Abraham grew up with the Rambam (Maimonides). They studied together and were good friends, but Rabbi Abraham never revealed his difficulties to his friend. However the Rambam, who was also very clever, felt his friend's poverty and lucklessness.

It is told that the Rambam and Rabbi Abraham Ibn-Ezra were born on the same day at the very same minute, but the Rambam was born when the Wheel of Fortune was at the top and Rabbi Abraham when it turned down.

Rabbi Abraham used to buy and sell goods, but the day after he bought them, their price would always go down. The Rambam used to help and advise him, but to no avail—Rabbi Abraham's luck was always upside down.

One day the Rambam decided to help his friend with a considerable sum of money. Knowing that Rabbi Abraham would not accept his direct help, he put a purse full of money near his friend's house at a place where the rabbi would pass on his way to the synagogue in the very early hours of the morning when no one was about yet.

That evening Rabbi Abraham Ibn-Ezra had been sitting and thinking: "I must not complain against my fate and poverty. How would it be if I were blind and could not walk! I must thank the Almighty that I am open-eyed, because it is better to be poor and open-eyed than rich and blind."

The next morning on his way to the House of Prayer he shut his eyes and said in his heart: "I shall try to walk with closed eyes as if I were blind." And so it was that he passed the purse of money without noticing it.

The Rambam saw that there was no change with his friend, and he asked him, "How are you? What did you do this morning?"

Rabbi Abraham answered, "Yesterday evening I sat and thought: How good it is that I am not blind and I am able to see and walk. This morning I went to the house of prayer as if I were blind, leaning against the wall. How miserable are those who cannot see."

Thus the Rambam realized that it is impossible to change the fate of a man born when the Wheel of Fortune is turned down.

· *11* · *The Blood Libel*

IFA 25. Recorded by Elisheva Schoenfeld in Affula in 1955 from Obadia Pervi, a laborer, born in Harie, a village in southeastern Yemen near Sadda.

This tale is a version of a widespread Jewish legend concerning false blood accusation. Motif V229.1, "Saint commands return from dead with supernatural information," specifically applies, and the general Motifs K2110, "Slanders," and V360, "Christian and Jewish traditions about each other," are present. Elijah the

Prophet is the most popular hero in Jewish folk legends, in which he often plays the role of a savior. For tales about him in the talmudic-midrashic literature, see L. Ginzberg, The Legends of the Jews, *VII, 133–35,* s. v. *"Elijah." This legend is usually connected with the Passover Night ("Seder"). For such associations, see Dov Noy, "Elijah the Prophet at the Seder Night" (Hebrew),* Machnayim, *No. 43 (1960), 100–106.*

E. Schoenfeld has written on "Judisch-orientalische Märchen-erzähler in Israel," in Internationaler Kongress der Volkserzäh-lungsforscher in Kiel und Kopenhagen, *ed. Kurt Ranke (Berlin, 1961), pp. 385–90.*

• MANY YEARS AGO there lived a king who dearly loved the Jews in his country. His ministers, however, were jealous of them and smitten by bitter envy. Thus they decided to disgrace the Jews, so that the king would no longer respect them.

One day, while the king's son was playing in the garden, he was approached by five men, who caught hold of him and carried him to the outskirts of the town. There they killed him and then brought his little body into the women's section of the synagogue.

When the king was informed that his little son had been found dead in the synagogue, he became very sad and angry. He called for the rabbi of the community and cried, "What have you done to me? All of you are guilty of the death of my child! I shall exterminate all the Jews in my kingdom!"

The rabbi asked the king for three days respite before carrying out his threat. He hoped by then to reveal the true facts and to expose the murderer. The king agreed. Whereupon the rabbi ordered all his subjects to fast, pray, and distribute alms until the guilty man had been detected.

That night in a dream the rabbi saw an old man who revealed what had really happened: the five ministers of the king had killed the child. The old man also taught him what to do the following day. That old man was, of course, no other than Elijah the Prophet.

The next day the rabbi went to the palace and asked the king to send for the body of his son. The body was brought to the palace. The rabbi put it on a table in the presence of the king and his ministers. He touched the child's forehead and then his own forehead with a stick. Thereupon he prayed to God, without paying attention to the happenings around him.

Suddenly the prince opened his eyes and sat up.

"Tell us how you were killed," the rabbi told him.

The boy opened his mouth and talked as if in a deep sleep: "I was playing in the garden, and these five men seized me!" he said, pointing his finger at them. "This one, this one, this one, and these two. They took me to the outskirts of the town. Then one of them drew out a knife. I cried very much and begged him not to kill me, but he paid no attention to my pleadings and stabbed me with his knife. My blood gushed out on all sides and splashed a large stone beside me."

When the boy had finished speaking, he closed his eyes and lay down. Once again he was lifeless.

The astounded king sent some of his soldiers to look for the stone stained with the boy's blood. They actually found it and brought it to the king. He at once gave orders that his five ministers should be killed. And he continued to revere the Jews of his kingdom until the end of his days.

·12· *The Reward of a Midwife*

IFA 279. Recorded by Mordechai Zahavi from a workman, born in Zakho, Iraqi Kurdistan.

Type 476*, In the Frog's House, contains Motif F372.1, "Fairies take human midwife to attend fairy woman." The appearance of a demon instead of a fairy is a common variation. See S. Thompson, The Folktale, p. 248. For a version in which a mohel (circumciser) appears in the same situation as the midwife, see M. Ben-Yehezkel, The Book of Tales (Hebrew), IV, 33–37. Motifs C242, "Tabu: eating food of witch (demon)," and F333, "Fairy grateful to human midwife," are common to both versions.

Type 476* has been reported only from Hungary. For Jewish *literary versions, see M. J. Bin Gorion,* Der Born Judas, *VI, 63–67, and for a Sephardic Jewish text, see M. Grunwald, "Spaniolic Tales and Their Motifs," No. 20.*

The opportunities of obtaining magic objects for deposit in folk museums, when folktale informants mention having such objects in their possession (as in the tale below), are discussed by Dov Noy, "Archiving and Presenting Folk Literature in an Ethnological Museum," Journal of American Folklore, *LXXV (1962), 23–28.*

• MY GRANDMOTHER, may she rest in peace, was a midwife. She carried on her work for the love of it, without seeking any reward. She was sure that her payment would be to go straight to Heaven. As there were neither doctors nor qualified midwives in Zakho, Kurdistan, at that time, my grandmother had her hands full.

One day she sat outside her house embroidering. She was very tired after a hard day's work. Suddenly she saw a beautiful cat creeping stealthily into the house, so that she could not be heard, and sniffing in all the corners as if she were searching for food.

The cat found favor with my grandmother, who fed her, noticing as she did so that the cat was pregnant! My grandmother said to herself, "If only I were this cat's midwife!"

Days passed, and one dark and stormy night my grandmother was awakened from sleep by the sound of steps. There was a rap at the door. She got up hurriedly, dressed, and opened the door. On the threshold someone stood, tired and sweating. He spoke hurriedly, "*Sotte* (Grandma), come with me, and you will earn a lot of money. My wife is with child and the pangs of birth are already with her. There is no one to help her."

Grandmother listened to the request, rejoicing with delight. This was simply a windfall at such an hour and on such a night. It would be like doing all the six hundred and thirteen commands at once.

Zakho is a small town, and Grandma strode up the main street behind the man. She could not understand why she did not hear his footsteps. Suddenly she noticed that they had gone beyond the last house in the town and were now walking in an open field. She trembled all over, knowing that no one lived there. She understood that the man, leading her, was no other than a *shed*.

"Lord, have mercy on me," she muttered to herself, but she did not utter a sound. They reached a stone bridge, with each stone ten meters square. They entered a huge cave, and therein Grandma heard a man's voice, "Grandmother, come in. It is here."

My grandmother became scared. Inside there were many *shedim* and *shedot*, with little horns on their heads, singing and mewing like cats.

"What a pleasant company in which to find myself," she thought to herself, but she did not say a word. The *shed* with the longest horns took her aside and said to her, "If the newborn is a son, you will get everything you want, but if it is a daughter, God forbid."

Pale with fear, Grandma did not answer a word. She entered the confinement room, and whom did she see? The cat that had visited her a little while ago was lying there. The cat opened her mouth and whispered, "Dear grandmother, do not eat here or you will be turned into a *shed*."

My grandmother kept in mind the cat's warning and did not eat anything in the cave during the whole night, although she was offered the best and most delicious foods and drinks. When the time of birth came, she rolled up her sleeves and set to work. A male cat was born. What rejoicing broke out in the cave! It reached the heavens! The chief of the *shedim* called my grandmother and said to her, "Whatever you ask even up to half of my kingdom, I will give you."

"No," said my grandmother, "I do not want anything. The price for a good deed is the deed itself."

"That is impossible! You must take something! This is our custom, and you cannot disregard it," said the chief, in a warning voice.

My grandmother was aware that this was not a joke. She saw a bunch of garlic in the corner of the room and asked for a little bit, just to get rid of the obligation. They stuffed her dress with garlic and then escorted her home.

Tired and broken, Grandma threw the garlic by the door and sank into her bed. The next morning her grandchild woke her up: "From where did you bring so much gold, Grandma?" She looked toward the door and saw that the garlic was nothing else than pure gold. She distributed the gold among her children, grandchildren, and all the family.

After many years she passed away, and her grandchildren are now scattered all over the world, I and my sister being privileged to live in Israel, the Holy Land. And each of us keeps until this day a piece of the golden garlic, the reward of our grandmother, the midwife, and her gift to us.

Part II
The Covetous

·13· No Escape from Fate

IFA 299. Recorded by Uri Baranes, a high-school student, from Avigdor Hadjadj, born in Libya.

Type 934, The Prince and the Storm. In this text Motif M341.2.5, "Prophecy: death by horse's head," is coupled with M370.1, "Prophecy of death fulfilled." This motif has been studied by Archer Taylor, in "The Death of Qrvar Oddr," Modern Philology, XIX (1921), 93–106. While 116 Irish texts are reported, the chief distribution is in eastern and southern Europe. Variants are known from central Asia: for Uzbekistan, see M. I. Shewerdin (ed.), Uzbekian Folktales Vol. I, No. 47, the third story; and for an Uighur text, see M. N. Kabirov and V. F. Shahmatov, Uigur Folktales No. 27. Jewish literary versions can be found in M. Gaster, The Exempla of the Rabbis, No. 140, pp. 85, 216, and M. Gaster (ed.), Ma'aseh Book, Vol. I, Nos. 16, 17, 81.

Two United States texts, collected in Michigan in 1954, are in the Indiana University Folklore Archives. In this modern form, a man forewarned of death by means of a horse on a certain day spends the day in bed; a picture of a horse drops from the wall and kills him.

• IN A CERTAIN TOWN there lived a very rich man who had many sons and many possessions. He enjoyed a life of luxury and pleasure. For all that, he was always beset by one fear: How will my riches help me in times of trouble? Who will save me from death?

The rich man spent his time thinking of the day of death and searching for ways to escape from it.

One day he consulted soothsayers, and for a big sum of money, they revealed to him the day of his death and the way he would encounter it. He would be trampled by a horse or an elephant.

The rich man thought he had found the way to save himself and to cheat the Angel of Death. Some months before he was doomed to die, he went far away to the heart of the desert, pitched a tent, and dwelt there with his wife. Their children re-

mained in the town and from time to time visited their father
and brought him food, drinks, and presents. So, with a light
heart, the rich man went on dwelling in his tent.

The day predicted by the soothsayer as the day of his death
came and passed. The following day the rich man cried out to
his wife in excitement, "The soothsayers have cheated me! They
predicted the day of my death just to gain fortune. I shall demand my money back."

His wife said to him, "Beware of them. Maybe the day of your
death has been postponed by heaven. Why do you want to
leave? Maybe a horse or an elephant will trample you on the
way."

The rich man remained in his tent in the heart of the desert
and did not go because he feared for his life.

Many months passed, and the man did not die. He thought
he had been forgotten by Heaven and had succeeded in cheating
Fate.

One day, in the heat of midday, the rich man and his wife
were sitting in the tent over their midday meal. Suddenly the
tent collapsed with the weight of a heavy eagle clutching a horse.
The eagle wanted to devour his heavy prey on the "green spot"
in the desert but the weak canvas broke down.

When the wife began to put up the tent, she found her husband
beneath it without a breath of life.

She wept with bitter tears and cried, "There is no escape from
Fate! There is no escape from Fate!"

·*14*· *The Spendthrift Son*

*IFA 411. Recorded by Zvulun Kort, as heard in Herat, Afghani-
stan, in his youth.*

Type 910D, The Treasure of the Hanging Man, *containing
Motifs L114.2, "Spendthrift hero," H1558.7, "Test of friendship:
the power of money," and H1558.7.2, "Friends desert when man
reports loss of his money." For Turkish versions of this type, see
W. Eberhard and P. N. Boratav, Typen turkischer Volksmärchen,*

No. 315, "Murteza"; and for Arabic literary treatments, see V. Chauvin, Bibliographie des ouvrages Arabes . . . , Vol. V, No. 63, p. 133, and Vol. VIII, No. 65, p. 94. A discussion of this tale is found in W. A. Clouston, Popular Tales and Fiction, II, 53–64.

Type 910D is reported from eastern and southern Europe, India, and Japan. Several versions are in the IFA.

• IN A CERTAIN Eastern country there lived a well-to-do merchant. He was a widower with an only son, a weak-willed spendthrift. The merchant was always busy; so he could not concern himself with his son's doings and life of revelry. Day after day the son used to arrange drinking bouts and to invite his young comrades to while away the time in wild merrymaking.

One day the merchant called his son and said, "My son, give up your life of pleasure and build your home. Your friends will not help you in the hour of need."

The son laughed and said, "My friends are faithful and devoted."

Several times the father warned his son, but to no avail. One day the old father took two massive hollow pillars, filled them with golden coins, and erected them in his courtyard. Then he called his son and said, "My son, I am about to die. When I advised you to build a house and work, you would not listen. The money I shall leave you will suffice for but a short time. When it is gone and you are hungry, do not beg for charity. I have erected two posts outside. Tie a rope to them, climb up, and hang yourself."

The son laughed at his father's strange advice.

The merchant died, and after a short time the son spent all his money. Then he approached his friends, "I have no more money, and I am no longer able to entertain you." On hearing this his friends said, "By all means we will invite you to our parties, even if you have no money, on condition that you cook the food."

The son had no choice but to agree. His friends bought rice and meat and sent him to the kitchen while they sat in the hall drinking and making merry. The young man was angry with his friends' conduct; however, he went to the kitchen, put on the pot, and lit the stove. He was tired and soon fell asleep. Meanwhile a dog entered the kitchen and ate up all the food. The young man awoke and found the pot empty. He went to his friends and told them what had happened. They did not believe him and beat him, calling him a liar. Then they threw him outside. He understood at last that his friends had deceived him and that his father had been right. Now there was no choice but to take his father's advice. He fixed the rope to the pillars and tried to hang himself. But the hollow pillars broke down, and gold and precious stones fell out and were scattered on the ground. When the son saw these treasures, he realized that his clever father had loved him and acted for his good and tried to spare his suffering. Thereupon he decided to give up his friends.

One day he told them that he had money again and invited them to a party. They were delighted, and all of them came to drink and to make merry. He showed them a precious stone and said, "Look, friends, what has happened to my stone. A rat nibbled it, and the stone has broken in two."

"True," said his friends, "a rat eats stones!"

The young man then asked, "If a rat eats stones, why cannot a dog eat meat?" He beckoned to a group of men waiting outside with sticks, and they set upon the guests and beat them up.

From that time on the young man mended his ways and began to work. He built a house and married. Sons and daughters were born to him, and he lived a life of happiness.

• *15* •   The Porter Who Lost His Appetite

IFA 44. Recorded by Elisheva Schoenfeld in Affula in 1956 from Mordechai "Marko" Litsi, born in Turkey.

Type 754, The Happy Friar, and Motif J1085.1, "The happy friar becomes unhappier as he receives even more and more money." A similar pattern is found in Type 836F*, The Miser and the Eye Ointment. For a different ending of this story, see N. Gross, Folktales and Parables, pp. 164–65. Type 754 is scattered throughout Europe and is known in China. The second part *of this story falls under Motifs J1149.5, "Detection of guilt by smile," K33, "Theft from blind person," and K2096.2, "Thief robs blind miser of his hoard and gives a tenth away in charity in form of a banquet to the poor." Cf. Type 1577*, Blind Robber Paid Back.*

A similar ending occurs in No. 18 (in this book), "The Shop-keeper and the Four Blind Beggars" (IFA 1856), in which the beggar chokes on bread bought with his own money (Motif V431, "Charity of usurer ineffective").

• MANY YEARS AGO there lived a load carrier. He earned his living by carrying heavy baggage on his back on a board of wood bound to his shoulders and padded with a cushion of straw. This porter always had an appetite, and whenever he had time, he used to eat in the street. He always ate at the same place, opposite the mansion owned by a rich man. When the rich man used to see the porter eating with a hearty appetite, he would wonder to himself: "How is it that this poor man eats and eats and always has a great appetite? How is it that he loves to eat so much? Why cannot I enjoy eating like that?"

One day the rich man met his friend, a rich merchant living in a mansion outside the town. He described the porter's lusty and unsatiated appetite. The merchant, surprised and dejected, said, "I eat very little. I simply have no appetite; the food sticks in my throat, and I am not able to swallow it. Let us see what happens to the porter when he becomes as rich as us!"

One of the men decided to invite the porter to his mansion and give him as much silver and gold as he desired. So the next day he approached the porter and said, "Friend, I have work for you; come with me to my house."

The porter took the board of wood on his shoulders, followed the rich man, and entered his mansion. The rich man took a bunch of keys and opened a door. The porter saw a room full of copper. Then the rich man opened the second room, and the porter saw a room full of silver. Finally, the rich man opened a third room, and the porter saw a room full of gold pounds. The porter asked the owner of the mansion, "Tell me, sir. You brought me here to work. What is there to do?"

"Take as much gold as you can carry. That is why I invited you to come here," answered the rich man.

The porter pulled off his long underpants and his long-sleeved vest and tied the openings of the pants and the sleeves. Then he filled up the garments with gold and went home. He arrived home, and from his underpants and vest he poured out the gold pounds into a clay jar. But the gold did not come up to the brim of the jar; there was still space for four fingers. Said the porter, in his heart: "I must fill this jar to the brim. I will not buy food or clothes and will scrape up every penny until I fill the jar." And so it was. He did not eat or buy new clothes for himself, his wife, or children.

One day the porter met the rich man who had given him the gold. The rich man was surprised: "Why has your face fallen so? Why have you lost weight?" he asked.

"I have no appetite," answered the porter. "I put the gold you gave me into a jar, but it was not enough to fill it up; there is still room there. I shall have no appetite until the jar is completely filled up!"

The rich man invited the porter to his house for the second time and said to him, "Bring the jar to my house, and fill it right up to the brim."

The porter took the jar and went to the rich man's mansion. As soon as he arrived there, the rich man snatched the jar from his hand and broke it into pieces. The gold scattered all over the floor.

"If you do not know what to do with the gold, you do not deserve to have it!" shouted the rich man in anger, giving the porter a clout on his leg. The porter rolled down the stairs and was blinded by a hard knock on his head.

The blind porter had no other way than to beg for alms. To everyone who gave him a penny he used to say, "Before you give me money, give me also a pinch, because I truly deserve it." And so every passer-by used to give him a penny and a pinch.

After the porter lost his sight, he was afraid to go back home. He wandered in the streets and the alleys of the town until he found a small empty hut where he used to sleep at night. Every evening on entering, he used to tap with his stick in every corner in order to feel if anyone was there. He dug a hole under a bench, and there he kept all the money he earned by begging. The beggar never spent money on food. He lived on the bread he was given by people who pitied him. And so time passed.

A thief noticed the blind beggar sitting day by day in the same place, and he thought to himself: "This man does not spend his money on food because all his needs are supplied to him. I wonder what he does with his money." One evening the thief followed the blind man, taking care that his presence was unnoticed. The thief entered the hut with the beggar, carefully avoiding the stick the blind man was tapping around the room. The thief saw the beggar's hole under the bench, filled with coins he had saved up for years. Next day, after the beggar left, the thief stole all the money.

In time the thief built himself houses, opened shops, and became a rich man.

One day the thief passed the blind man and wanted to give him a penny and a roll. "Before you give me money, pinch me!" ordered the blind man according to his custom.

The thief did as he was bidden, and afterwards he gave the blind man a roll. The blind man wanted to eat it but the roll stuck in his throat, and he spat it out. Then he pushed the thief and began to shout in a loud voice, "Thief, thief!" Immediately, a large crowd gathered around, and the police took the two of them away for investigation.

"This is the man who stole all my savings!" cried the blind man.

"How do you know, if you cannot see?" he was asked. The blind man explained, "The roll this man gave me was bought with my own money. It must have been, because it stuck in my throat, and never could I eat bread bought with my money."

They did not believe him and bought two rolls, one with the policeman's money and one with the thief's money. The blind man ate the roll bought with the policeman's money and swallowed it without difficulty. But when they gave him the roll bought with the thief's money, he was not able to swallow it, for the roll stuck in his throat, choking him. The police saw that the words of the blind man were true, and the thief was arrested. He confessed his guilt and returned to the blind man all the money he had taken from him. The blind man went to a doctor, had an operation, and his sight was restored.

·16· A Man with Many Court Cases

IFA 1795. Recorded by Heda Jason from Zvi Galil, who heard the story from a Bokharan shoemaker.

Type 1534, Series of Clever Unjust Decisions (the corresponding Motif is J1173, "Series of clever unjust decisions: plaintiff voluntarily withdraws") is very common in Oriental folklore. IFA versions of the tale were recorded from Yemenite and Afghanistan Jews. Cf. also W. Eberhard–P. N. Boratav, No. 296, "Der bestechliche Richter." Variants from Palestinian Arabs are in Abu Naaman, On the Way to the Land of Happiness *(Hebrew), Nos. 15 and 42, and C. G. Campbell,* Told in the Market Place, *pp. 40–43; and a Jewish text from eastern Europe is in N. Gross, p. 270.*

Type 1534 is known in the Mediterranean countries, Spanish America, and India.

• ONCE THERE was a man who owed a large sum of money, a hundred pounds, which he was not able to pay. A year passed, and the lender approached him, demanding the money back. The man did not have it; so a quarrel broke out which led to a fight. The borrower ran away, chased by the money lender. They ran and they ran, until suddenly the debtor fell from a roof, crushing an old man sitting below.

The son of the old man shouted, "You have killed my father!"

The borrower ran off quickly, and now two men were close on his heels. He ran and ran until he tripped over a pregnant woman, causing her a miscarriage. The woman's husband got up, and he too joined in the chase. Faster and faster the borrower ran. Suddenly he lost his balance. So he caught hold of a donkey's tail, wrenching it off. The owner of the donkey dismounted, and he too gave chase. The borrower continued to run until he came to the cadi. He rushed inside his house at a great speed and found the cadi making love to his servant girl.

"I have caught you, cadi!" shouted the borrower.

The cadi immediately tried to smooth over the matter. "I will settle your case, if you hold your tongue."

In the meantime the accusers arrived on the scene. First to enter was the moneylender, shouting, "This man owes me a hundred pounds which he refuses to pay!"

"What! Cannot you see that he is unable to pay? How can you demand money from him! Pay a hundred pounds fine! Immediately!"

"But . . . ," the man began to argue.

"No buts, or you will be imprisoned."

The man hurriedly paid the fine and went off.

The second man entered and pointed to the borrower. "He killed my father!" He wept and told what had happened.

"Well," said the cadi, and he ordered the son of the dead man thus: "Now you climb on the roof and jump down on this man, who will stand below. 'Measure for measure' is the essence of justice."

"But my cadi! What if I am killed?"

"If you do not agree, pay a fine of a hundred pounds."

The man had no choice. He paid the fine and went off.

The pregnant woman's husband entered and told how the runaway had tripped over his wife, causing her miscarriage.

"Well," said the cadi. "Put your wife at his disposal till she is pregnant again."

"What? My wife?"

"If you do not agree, pay a fine of a hundred pounds."

Of course the man paid the fine and went off. What else could he do? The fourth man entered.

"Have you anything to say?" asked the cadi.

"I have nothing to say, sir. My donkey never had a tail. I swear."

·17· The Landlord and His Son

IFA 1913. Recorded by M. Glass from his Lithuanian-born grand-mother.

Type 837, How the Wicked Lord Was Punished. This tale type is reported mainly from eastern Europe, having been found no farther west than Sweden and Italy. One version has been collected from West Indies Negroes, and two are known in India. The largest number of texts (fifteen) comes from Lithu-ania. A Jewish variant from eastern Europe is in N. Gross, pp. 362–63, and one from Sephardic Jews in Morocco is in A. D. L. Palacin, Cuentos Populares de los Judios . . . , *No. 18.*

• MANY YEARS AGO in a small hut within a forest in Lithuania there lived a gentle old woman. Many thought that she was a witch. She lived on mushrooms and on water from the well close by. She did not like human company and used to repeat all the time a single sentence, "One day you will find yourself." Nobody knew the meaning of these words.

The old woman often paid visits to a Polish landlord in the neighboring village. From time to time he gave her some food. In the course of time the landlord began to hate the old woman, and one day he decided to get rid of her. He baked for her a beautiful cake but put within it some poison.

That day the landlord talked with his guest in a very friendly fashion, and the conversation went longer than usual. The old woman whispered again and again, "One day you will find your-self."

"Yes," thought the cunning man within his heart, "shortly she will find herself or the Angel of Death will find her." And he de-livered the cake to the old woman. "Such a cake you have never tasted before," he assured her.

The old woman took the cake, thanked the merciful host, and went home.

On the same day that the old woman visited the landlord, his young son participated in a big hunt in the woods. He and his servants lost their way and so came across the hut where the old woman lived. He told her how thirsty and hungry he was, and she invited him to have a piece of cake, which she had not yet touched. The young man fell down after his first bite. When the servants saw the master dead, they sent immediately for the father. Only then, when the landlord fell down on his son's body weeping bitterly, did he understand what the old woman's words meant—"One day you will find yourself."

You see how true is the Jewish proverb, "The man who makes holes falls into them himself" (Psalms 7:16).

·18· The Shopkeeper and the Four Blind Beggars

IFA 1856. Recorded by Zvulun Kort, as heard in his youth in Afghanistan.

A variation of Type 1577*, Blind Robber Paid Back. Cf. Motifs K306.4, "Blind man steals from neighbor who in turn steals from him," and K333, "Theft from blind person." A similar ending employing Motif V431, "Charity of usurer ineffective," is present in No. 15 (in this book), "The Porter Who Lost His Appetite" (IFA 44). Type 1577* is reported only from Estonia, Slovenia, and Turkey (W. Eberhard-P. N. Boratav, No. 345, "Die Blinden als Diebe"). A version originating with Sephardic Jews is in M. Grunwald, No. 49.

• A BLIND BEGGAR used to go to the market and beg for alms. Whatever he collected he used to hide in a hut outside the town. One day he approached one of the shops in the market. The shopkeeper did not have any small money; so he asked the blind man to give him change. The blind man assented, whereupon the shopkeeper gave him a big coin. The blind man fingered the coin, put it in his trousers, and began to walk out. The shopkeeper called after him and said, "Please give me the change."

The blind man began to shout that the shopkeeper not only had not given him alms but was also accusing him of stealing. People gathered around them and took the part of the blind man. The shopkeeper had no choice. He accepted the situation but followed the blind man. He saw him enter his hut, dislodge a brick, and hide all the money he had collected during the day in the hole underneath it. The shopkeeper waited outside until the blind man left. Then he entered the hut, raised the brick, took all the coins underneath it, and went away. When the blind man came back, he did not find the coins and shouted bitterly, "Alas! I am lost."

The blind man went to his friend, who was also blind, and began crying and shouting bitterly. His friend asked, "What is the matter?"

"All the money which I have saved till now has been stolen."

"How did it happen? Where did you keep your money?"

"Under a brick in my hut."

His friend said in astonishment, "How could you keep money under a brick?"

"Why not? Where should one keep money? What place is safer?"

"Here is an old stick of mine," said his friend. "Even if it were left in the street, no one would notice it. That's where I keep my money."

Meanwhile the shopkeeper had been following the blind man, and he overheard the conversation. As the blind man stretched out his stick, the shopkeeper caught it and moved aside. A little while later the blind man asked for his stick. His blind friend was surprised, "Which stick?"

The owner of the stick answered him angrily, "You came here to cheat me and to steal my money!" They began to hit each other. Then they went to a third blind man; the shopkeeper continued to follow them, but they were not aware of his presence.

They related to the third blind man how the first one's coins had disappeared from under the stone and how he had come to cheat his comrade and had taken his stick full of coins.

The third blind man said: "You are stupid. Is that the way to keep money, under a stone or in a stick? Now here is my shirt;

I always wear it and never take it off my back." While speaking he took off his shirt and stretched it out to them. Immediately the shopkeeper caught hold of the shirt and moved aside.

The third blind man began to search and ask for his shirt while the other two said, "Which shirt?"

The third blind man began to shout and cry, and they all decided to go to another blind man, the fourth. All the time the shopkeeper kept following them. They approached the fourth blind man and began to recount all their stories.

The third blind man was shouting and crying that the other two had cheated him and stolen all his money. The fourth blind man said: "Is this the way to keep money, under a stone? in a stick? in a shirt? Here I have a body warmer, a woven bag five centimeters broad. It is made like a belt and I put my money inside and fasten it round my thighs. While talking he took off the warmer and stretched it out to his friends. The shopkeeper caught hold of the warmer and moved aside.

After a while the fourth blind man felt around for his warmer. "Which warmer?" shouted the other three blind men. "Why are you accusing us?"

Again they began to quarrel and hit each other. Then the fourth blind man shouted, "For sure, a man who can see is following us and getting hold of our money." The four of them decided to beg for alms and then to divide the collection among themselves. And so they did. They went round the streets of the town and the market begging and divided their money amongst them.

One day they passed the shop of the man who had cheated them. He took pity on them and gave them a big coin. The blind men were astonished. "What was the reason?" Then they thought, "Maybe this was the man who took our money." "What shall we do?" said one of them. "It so happens that by nature I cannot eat anything I buy with my own money. It sticks in my throat." Then they bought bread and grapes and sat down to eat. But the one man simply could not swallow his food. Now they were sure that this shopkeeper had got hold of their money. The four of them went to the shopkeeper and began to shout, "Return our money!"

Meanwhile people gathered around, and soon the police appeared and took the blind men and the shopkeeper to the police station. There the four blind men told how a stranger had grabbed their money. One of them said that he was unable to swallow food bought with his own money and that he had not been able to swallow the food bought with the money the shopkeeper had given him.

Then the shopkeeper told his story. Once a blind man had passed by his shop. He had given the man money, but having only a big coin, he had asked him for change, but the blind man had hidden the coin. "When I asked him for change, he began to shout that I wanted to rob him. Men came and took his side. So I decided to follow him. When we came to his place, I saw him hiding his money, and afterwards I took it. Then I was curious to know what he was going to do and followed him farther. Then I took all of their money."

The policeman ordered the shopkeeper to give the money back to the blind men, and so it was.

·*19*· *The Rich Beggar and His Wonderful Purse*

IFA 609. Recorded by A. Alkalaj from his Bulgarian-born mother.

An unusual ending to Type 580*, The Inexhaustible Purse, and Motif D1451, "Inexhaustible purse furnishes money," is here provided by Motif C930, "Loss of fortune for breaking tabu." Also central is Motif G303.9.8.5, "Gold causes man to become miser." Only two Finnish-Swedish texts are reported for Type 580*.

• THERE WAS once a poor peasant. One day he came home from the fields, tired and exhausted. He lay down on his bed and begged God for just a little treasure. He pleaded and pleaded, and then all of a sudden he caught sight of a little purse lying near his feet. A heavenly voice said to him, "Take this purse as a gift from God. You will find a single coin inside, and the moment you take it out, another coin will take its place. On no account spend the money until you have thrown the purse into the river. Then the purse will be transformed into a fish, and the money into fins."

The peasant was delighted, and all that night and the following day he took one coin after another from that purse. By the next evening he had succeeded in gathering a full sack of coins. Next day there was no bread left in the house, but the peasant would not spend a single coin to buy food for himself.

"I will gather another sack of money and only then throw my gift into the river."

That day he asked a neighbor for bread and on the following day went out to beg for alms in the streets because, as he said, "It won't do me any harm if I fill another sack with coins before I spend the money and throw the wonderful purse into the river." And so it happened time and time again. Every day he went out to beg for alms in order to support himself and not spend any of his money. Afterward he pulled out coins from his purse again. Many times he took his purse to the river, intending to throw it in, but whenever he reached the riverbank, he decided to put it off until he had collected just one more sack of coins.

So he continued to gather coins until the end of his days, never spending anything because he did not want to part with his wonderful purse. He died very rich, and his home was filled with sacks of coins, but not a mouthful of food was to be found there.

.20. *The Beggar and His Ass*

IFA 209. Recorded by Lea Ben-Gershon from her grandmother, born in Iraq.

Type 751C*, Wealth Leads to Pride, is popular in the Orient. The central motif of this tale, B103.1.1, "Gold-producing ass: droppings of gold," is often part of Type 563, The Table, the Ass, and the Stick"; for further references, see the headnote to No. 21 (in this book), "The Coffeemill, the Tray, and the Stick" (IFA 352). Additional bibliography on gold-producing animals can be found in the Motif-Index of Folk-Literature, by Stith Thompson, under Motif B103, "Treasure-producing animals," and in

N. M. Penzer (ed.), The Ocean of Story, *V, 11, n. 1. The present ending with Motif Q281, "Ingratitude punished," is unusual in this tale type. For parallels to this ending, see M. Gaster,* The Exempla of the Rabbis, *No. 319, pp. 116, 239.*

Type 751C* is reported six times from Lithuania and once from Russia. For versions from central Asia, see M. I. Shewerdin, Vol. II, No. 150, and for one reported from Ossetia in the Caucasus, see A. H. Bjazirov, Ossetian Folktales, *No. 37.*

• MANY, MANY YEARS AGO, there was a poor beggar who used to wander around the streets and beg for alms. One day he was going on his way when he met an old fortuneteller, and he related to him the story of his life.

Said the fortuneteller, "Here is my ass. Take it! When you say to him, 'My ass, my ass, prove your power,' he will show his power, and you will become very rich. But bear in mind one thing: When you are rich, be kindhearted and do not mistreat your servants."

The beggar took the ass and rode cheerfully on his way. When he reached a certain spot, he turned to his ass and cried out, "My ass, my ass, prove your power!" Suddenly he heard the clink of coins and saw gold and silver scattered on the ground. With a happy heart, he collected the money. In time he rented a fine apartment with all the conveniences and acquired servants and maids.

Time went on, and the man no longer paid heed to the fortuneteller's warning and his own promise. He treated his servants with an iron hand. He was always shouting at them and was never satisfied with their work.

One day the man's ass was stolen, and he became sad and depressed. At last he went in search of the fortuneteller. He found him and told him his troubles.

This time the old man had no mercy and said, "Shame upon you. You oppressed your servants. From now on you will be a poor man."

And so it was. Again the man was forced to wander around the streets and to beg for alms.

· 21 · The Coffeemill, the Tray, and the Stick

IFA 352. Recorded by Yehuda Mazuz, a young worker, from his mother, Mas'uda Mazuz, born in Tunisia.

Type 563, The Table, the Ass, and the Stick. IFA versions of this type have been collected from Turkish, Tunisian, and Iraqi Jews. Thus far this version reported in Israel is the first one of Tunisian origin. Cf. No. 20 (in this book), "The Beggar and His Ass" (IFA 209), from Iraq. Antti Aarne analyzed this tale type in his monograph "Die Zaubergaben," Journal de la Société Finno-ougrienne, XXVII (1909), 1–96, and for further discussion, see K. Krohn, "Ubersicht über einige Resultate der Märchenforschung" (Folklore Fellows Communications, No. 96 [1931]), pp. 48–53. The tale is found in the Grimms' collection, No. 36, "The Wishing-Table, the Golden Ass and the Cudgel in the Sack"; bibliographical references can be found in J. Bolte and G. Polívka, Anmerkungen zu den Kinder und Hausmärchen der Brüder Grimm, I, 346–61. A Turkish version is given in W. Eberhard-P. N. Boratav, No. 176, "Tischleindeckdich I."

This international tale is reported from India, Africa, and throughout Europe, as well as from French, English, and Spanish traditions in America, where it has also passed into circulation among the Indians. Recently published Asian versions are given in Shewerdin, Vol. I, No. 24, and Vol. II, No. 131 (Uzbekian); Bjazirov, No. 17 (Ossetian); and Bgazhda, No. 8 (Abhazian). A Palestinian Arab example is in Abu Naaman, No. 8, and a Sephardic Jewish one in Palacin, No. 67.

• ONCE THERE lived a poor woodcutter who had a wife and seven daughters. He worked very hard but nevertheless remained very poor. Thus many years went by.

Once, while felling trees, he suddenly saw a black man standing before him and asking him, "Why do you cut my head every day?"

The woodcutter's answer was, "Sir, I have at home a wife and seven daughters to feed. Felling trees is my only way of earning money. I sell the wood so we do not die from hunger, although we still starve."

The Negro's heart was filled with pity. He said, "I shall give you a coffeemill which will produce as much food as you wish. And do not come here any more."

The woodcutter cried for joy, kissed the Negro, praised and thanked him. He took his cutting implements and the coffeemill and returned home. On his way he rested, and being hungry, he decided to try out the mill. He said, "Mill, mill, give me meat, rice, and bread." And saying this, he closed his eyes. When he opened them, he found the food before him. He finished the meal and went hastily home.

He told his family in a joyful voice about the appearance of the Negro and his wonderful gift. All the family thanked God in heaven for his mercy and providence. Immediately, they wished for a good and hearty meal. And there it was.

So they lived happily for a whole week.

In their neighborhood there lived an old woman who visited them from time to time. One day, a week after the woodcutter brought home the mill, she visited them and asked as usual, "How are things?"

One of the daughters boasted, "Very good. Father does not work any more. We have a wonderful mill, providing whatever we wish."

So the old woman decided to acquire this mill for herself. One day she visited them again, when another daughter was at home. She asked for their coffeemill as she wanted to grind some coffee grains and had no mill. "I shall return the mill in about three hours," she promised. So she was given the mill. Of course, instead of returning the miraculous mill, she brought back an ordinary one, though it looked just the same as the woodcutter's mill.

The father returned in the evening, addressed his mill in the usual way, but alas! The mill did not work. The daughters told him about the old woman's visit, and the father gave them a very thorough beating. That night they ate the leftovers of their previous meal, and next day the woodcutter took his working implements and again went into the woods to cut trees.

He started to cut the first tree—and, again, who appeared? None other than the black man! And he addressed the woodcutter, "Did not I give you a wonderful mill in order to stop you from coming here? Why are you cutting my head again?"

The woodcutter answered, "Sir, my foolish daughters gave the mill to an old woman, and she did not return it. So I must work again."

The Negro thought for a while and said, "I am giving you a second chance. Here is a tray which will produce as much money as you wish. But do not return here anymore."

Joy filled the woodcutter's heart again. On his way he tried out the tray: "Tray, tray, give me money!" And there were coins of gold and silver. Again he told his wife and daughters about his second encounter with the Negro, and again all of them blessed God in heaven for his mercy and goodness. This time the woodcutter warned all of them not to lend the tray to any neighbor.

A week passed in happiness and abundance, and then the old woman came again for a visit. And once more the woodcutter was not at home. Treacherously, she led the woodcutter's wife and daughters into conversation, and you well know how talkative women are and how they love gossip! And believe it or not, when she left the woodcutter's house, she carried off the borrowed tray in her hands.

Imagine the father's anger when he returned home. He almost died of rage. Excuses like "the woman confused our heads" were of no avail. The wife and the daughters were thoroughly beaten, as they rightly deserved. And next morning the woodcutter took his working implements and again went into the woods.

He started to cut the first tree—and, again, who appeared? Of course, none other than the black man! The woodcutter told him the whole story, and the Negro said, "I gave you two chances, and you spoiled them. Here is your last chance. I am going to give you this stick. If it is near a person without clothing, it beats him until you say to the stick 'Enough'! First, beat yourself up, then your wife and daughters, and then the old woman your neighbor."

The woodcutter returned home, took off his clothes, and got a thorough beating, until he ordered "Enough"! Then he told his wife and daughters, "Today I have a wonderful thing for you. It is a stick which provides very good things. One by one you will enter the room and take off your clothes." The women were very happy. One by one they entered the room, took off their clothing, and were thoroughly beaten until the father ordered "Enough"!

The next day the old woman again came for a visit and asked her usual question, "How are things?" Of course she was told about the wonderful stick. When she left the house, she carried the stick with her.

A few days passed, and the old woman did not return. So they went to visit her, broke into her house, and found her dead. They understood well what had happened. The woman did not know how to stop the stick; so she was beaten to death. Of course, they found their mill and tray there and took both of them home.

Ever afterward they lived in happiness and abundance.

·22· *A Miser and a Generous Man*

IFA 654. Recorded by Varda Hilel, an elementary-school teacher, from her father, Shimon Hilel, a laborer, born in Tunisia.

A fine version of Type 613, The Two Travelers (Truth and Falsehood), episodes II, III, and IV. The contrast between the Motifs W152, "Stinginess," Q276, "Stinginess punished," and Q42, "Generosity rewarded," gives a moralistic coloring to this tale. For Jewish versions of this type from the homiletic literature, based on religious opposition, see M. Gaster, The Exempla of the Rabbis, Nos. 29, 110, 447; Gaster, Studies and Texts, II, 917–18; Gaster (ed.), Maʻaseh Book, No. 120; M. J. Bin Gorion, Der Born Judas, II, 197.

In Europe this tale is found in the Grimms' collection as No. 107, "The Two Travelers"; and for bibliography see J. Bolte-G. Polívka, II, 468–82. It is the subject of a monograph by Reidar Th.

Christiansen, The Tale of the Two Travellers (*Folklore Fellows Communications,* No. 24 [*Harmina, 1916*]). *S. Thompson discusses the story at length in* The Folktale, *pp. 80–81, commenting on its antiquity of some fifteen hundred years in Chinese and Hebrew writings and its modern dispersion from central Africa to Nova Scotia and Jamaica.*

In central Asia the tale is reported from Uzbekistan (M. I. Shewerdin, Vol. I, No. 43, and Vol. II, No. 152) and from Kazakhstan (W. Sidelnikov, No. 53). Texts from the Middle East can be found in S. Britajev and K. Kasbekov, Ossetian Folktales, *No. 11 (Caucasus); E. S. Stevens,* Folktales of Iraq, *No. 46 (Iraq); W. Eberhard–P. N. Boratav, Nos. 67, 253 (Turkey); H. Schmidt and P. Kahle,* Volkserzählungen aus Palästina, *No. 70 (Palestinian-Arab); and cf. N. Gross, pp. 36–37 (Jewish-eastern Europe).*

A similar ending with Motif N471, "Foolish attempt of second man to overhear secrets," occurs in No. 23 (in this book), "The Mountain of the Sun" (IFA 1637).

• THERE WAS A certain grocery shop belonging to two partners: one was a miser and one a generous man. Whenever the miser used to weigh sugar, flour, or any other food, he always took away a quantity from the scales, while the generous man always added to the scales.

"Why do you do it?" asked the miser.

"Because it is forbidden to steal, and in the future, too, I shall continue adding to the scales," came the answer.

"If that is so, we will split up, each of us working for himself from now on," decided the miser. Whereupon they both settled their accounts, each one receiving his share. The miser received the shop laden with goods, and the generous man the money. He decided in his heart, "I shall not live in this stingy man's town." He took money and food with him for the way and set off.

In those days there were no trains or cars, and people used to go from place to place on foot. The generous man was out in the open for days and nights; by day he walked, and by night he slept in a field. At last he arrived at a certain town, and when he drew near its walls, night fell. He said in his heart, "I shall sleep here for the night, and tomorrow I shall enter the town." Catching sight of a nearby pit lined with straw, he crept inside. In the night, sons of *shedim* held a meeting near the pit.

"Do you know, friends, what has happened in the nearby city?" one of them asked. "A king whose son is very ill lives there, and all the doctors have given up hope of saving him."

"He will live because I have a remedy," cried out one *shed*.

"What is the remedy?" asked one of them.

"The remedy is to take some oil, heat it, and rub the son's body. At once he will get up, sound and well."

In the morning the generous man entered the city and found it in mourning. He asked passers-by, "Why are you mourning?"

"The king's son is very ill," came the answer. "The king has proclaimed that if the child dies, he will give orders to kill every child of the same age as his son, as well as every child bearing the same name."

"Do not worry. I have a remedy!" said the newcomer.

Hearing this, the townsmen took him to the king saying, "Our lord and king! Here is a man who is ready to cure your son."

"Are you ready to cure my son?" asked the king in astonishment.

"Indeed, I am," came the answer.

"If you succeed, I shall make you greater than all the citizens in my state," declared the king. He brought the guest to the child's room. The man warmed some oil and rubbed the child's body with it. Immediately the child stood up on his feet, sound and healthy.

The king was overjoyed and ordered those who loved him to bestow a gift on the man who cured his son. Half an hour went by, and with the many gifts, the man became wealthier than he had ever been before in his life. He opened a big shop, and people came from near and far to buy provisions because the prices were very low.

The stingy man heard of that shop in the far-off country where goods were sold so cheaply, and he decided to go and buy there. Of course the two partners recognized each other. The miser asked, "How did you get so much money?"

"Stay here as my guest for seven days, and then I shall tell you the story," retorted the generous man.

The miser agreed. Seven days passed by, and the miser was told of the straw-lined pit and of all that had befallen his former partner. The stingy man decided to do as the generous man had done. "Look after my money until I return from the pit," he said.

Three days passed, and the *shedim* held another meeting near the pit. Before it began, one of them said, "We must not talk too much. The day has eyes, and the night has ears."

The *shedim* did not understand this, and he explained, "Do you remember the king's sick son? Here in this very well I revealed the remedy; but someone hiding inside overheard it and cured the boy."

One of the *shedim* got up and said, "Give me a match to search the pit." Then lo! What did he see? A man—the miser, of course —lying there. The *shed* lit the straw, and the man was burned. May all stingy men have the same fate!

Of course, as you have already guessed, all the miser's money was left with the generous man.

.23. *The Mountain of the Sun*

IFA 1637. Recorded by Menashe Razi, a young worker, from Isaac Gribi, born in Iraq.

Motifs B562.1.3, "Birds show man treasure," F752.1, "Mountain of gold," J2415, "Foolish imitation of lucky man," K41, "Plowing contest," and N471, "Foolish attempt of second man to overhear secrets," are substituted in this tale for equivalent motifs in IFA 654, Type 613, The Two Travelers, (see No. 22 in this book, "A Miser and a Generous Man"). However, the two tales form the same pattern, which is discussed in A. Dundes, "The Binary Structure of 'Unsuccessful Repetition' in Lithuanian Folktales," Western Folklore, XXI (1962), 165–73.

• ONCE THERE WERE two brothers. The elder brother was a miser. A stingy envious man was he, always chasing after money. All his life he yearned to gain the whole of his father's possessions. His younger brother was different. He was a good honest man, upright in his ways, and very fond of his brother. At last their father passed away, leaving his sons all his possessions: fields, vineyards, and many sheep and cattle. The days of mourning went by, and then the elder son approached his younger brother and cunningly said to him, "The time has come for us to divide our father's inheritance between us. Let us go to plow the fields tomorrow morning, and he who succeeds in plowing the larger area will inherit all. But one condition—it is forbidden that either of us should eat or drink during the whole day." The younger brother, who always heeded his elder brother, agreed to the plan. The following day the elder brother arose early, before sunrise, and while his younger brother was still sleeping, his wife prepared breakfast. He ate his fill, and after feeling his stomach, he got up and approached the younger brother's bed to awaken him.

"It is morning, my brother, and time to get up. Let's go to the fields!"

The younger brother jumped out of bed and dressed hurriedly. Without eating or drinking, he took his plowshare and followed his brother to the field, whereupon they both began to plow. The elder brother worked with speed and energy, while the younger brother worked slowly. The plow was heavy in his hands because he was hungry. That same evening their father's inheritance—the fields, vineyards, sheep, and cattle—passed over to the elder brother, while the younger brother remained without anything.

The next day the younger brother left the house and went to the mountains to search for his daily bread. He found a place to sleep in a hollow of a rock and became a woodcutter. He used to chop down trees and take the wood to town to sell, and with these scant earnings he bought bread and meat. His days passed in poverty, and in the meantime the elder brother prospered and became rich. He bought more fields and vineyards and built houses. By now he had forgotten his brother, whose share of the inheritance he had stolen.

One day the younger brother went out as usual to fell trees in the forest. As he approached a certain tree, to fell it with his ax, he raised his eyes to the treetop and saw among the branches a bird's nest. He took a stick and threw it over the nest, once, twice, and thrice, but each time he missed the mark. At last a raven flew from the nest, curled in the air over the woodcutter, fluttered his wings, and suddenly called out, "Do not destroy my nest. I built it for my soft nestlings with hard work. Do not destroy my home, and in return I shall take you to the Mountain of the Sun."

"What is there on the Mountain of the Sun?" asked the younger brother.

"Many treasures," answer the raven.

"And what are the treasures?" continued the younger brother suspiciously.

To this the raven answered, "Come to me tomorrow morning early, before sunrise. Take a small bag with you, and when you go to the Mountain of the Sun, you will see what treasures are there."

"Very well," said the younger brother and turned to another tree.

Next morning before sunrise, the younger brother took a small bag and followed the raven to the Mountain of the Sun. When they reached the mountain peak, the younger brother stood in astonishment and wonder, not believing his own eyes. Nuggets of gold, diamonds, and precious stones were lying on the ground, shining and sparkling to dazzle the eyes.

"Do not wait," said the raven. "Take your fill, and go before sunrise."

The younger brother did not stay long. He filled his little bag with gold, diamonds, and precious stones, thanked the raven, and then set off for his mountain dwelling. The same day he left the mountains and returned to his home town. He built a beautiful house there, bought fertile fields, and lived a happy life.

When it became known to the elder brother how his younger brother had gained his riches, he envied him very much. He could find no rest for his soul, until one fine day he took a big stick and ran to the forest. There in the forest he found the raven's nest and began to throw the stick toward it: once, twice, and thrice, but each time he missed the mark. At last the raven jumped out of the nest and began to plead, "Please, do not destroy my nest. I built it for my soft nestlings with hard work. If you pay heed to my plea, I shall take you tomorrow, before sunrise, to the Mountain of the Sun. Take with you a small bag and a grain of rice and be ready before sunrise."

"I shall come tomorrow," called the elder brother and ran home.

On entering his house he said to his wife, "Take the biggest sheet you have in the house and sew it into a sack. In his mind he thought that a little bag would not be large enough to take as many treasures from the Mountain of the Sun as he could load on his shoulders.

During the whole night the man and his wife were busy sewing the sack and in the morning, as the night mist began to lift, the elder brother followed the raven to the Mountain of the Sun. When they reached the peak of the mountain and the elder brother saw the gold nuggets, the dazzling diamonds, and the precious stones, the whole world was forgotten in his heart, and he fell upon the treasures and began to fill his huge sack. With great greed he grabbed the golden nuggets and precious stones, and he stuffed into his sack whatever came his way, trying to fill it to the very top.

"Enough, enough, do not lag behind," warned the raven. "Run home quickly or the sun will rise and scorch you with its blazing rays."

The elder brother did not listen. He wanted to fill his huge sack to the very top. He stretched himself on the ground and continued to collect more and more treasures. At last the sun rose with its burning rays and scorched the elder brother so that he was turned into a pile of ashes. The raven fluttered his wings and called out, "This is the end of a man who desired to take everything for himself." Then the raven stretched his wings and fled to his nest.

The younger brother continued to lead a happy and contented life until the end of his days.

• 24 • The Tall Tale of the Merchant's Son

IFA 7. Recorded by Elisheva Schoenfeld in Affula in 1955 from Mordechai "Marko" Litsi of Turkey.

This is an elaborate version of Type 1920, Contest in Lying, with an incident belonging to Type 1960G, The Great Tree. Fifteen Turkish versions are cited in W. Eberhard–P. N. Boratav,

No. 358, "Keloğlan *und der Müller.*" *Type 1920 has been brought from Europe to the New World in the French, Spanish, and English traditions. Two Japanese texts are given in R. M. Dorson,* Folk Legends of Japan (*Tokyo and Rutland, Vt., 1962*), *pp. 206–7.*

• MANY YEARS AGO there was a terrible war in a certain land, and so there was nothing to eat. At that time a rich merchant of the country died and bequeathed all his wealth to his only son. He left him a will ending with the following words: "Never do business with a man whose face is hairless."

There was a sack of wheat in the merchant's house, and the son decided to have it ground at the mill and to bake bread for himself and his children. He went to the mill and knocked at the door, and the miller opened it. In a trice the merchant's son noticed that the miller had a hairless face. Remembering his father's will, he said to the miller, "Good-by!" and went on to the second mill. There, too, a man whose face was hairless opened the door, and again the merchant's son went on his way. He reached the third mill, and the door was again opened by another miller with a hairless face.

So the merchant's son had no choice but to ask the third miller to grind his wheat. The hairless miller ground the wheat into flour, and when he handed the sack to the merchant's son, he begged that he might take a little to bake bread for his own children. "For quite a long time we have had no flour in the house," lamented the miller.

The merchant's son agreed to give him the flour. Thereupon the miller brought a basin, poured a little of the flour into it and added water. The dough was too thin; so the miller asked for a little more flour. Then the dough became too dry; so the miller added more water. He added too much, and the mixture became watery, and again the miller asked for a little flour. And so it went on until the sack of flour was empty. At the end the miller took the dough to the bakery and baked a big loaf of bread for himself.

When the merchant's son saw that the miller had cheated him, he remembered his father's will. He thought for a minute and then said to the miller, "You took all my flour and nothing remains for my children. Let each of us tell a tall tale, and he who tells the better one will get the loaf of bread."

The miller agreed and began to tell his tale: "My father was a peasant. Once he planted watermelons, but only one sprang up. It was so big that it covered the whole city. Highways had to be forced through it; otherwise, neither a horse nor a cart could pass by. For many months the watermelon lay in the city because there was no way to remove it."

Now it was the turn of the merchant's son, and this was the tale he told: "My grandfather was a beekeeper. One day a queen bee was missing from the hive. For many days he searched for the queen until he found her with a peasant, yoked with an ox to a plow. 'This is the queen of my hive!' he said to the peasant. 'Free her for me at once.' The peasant pleaded with the beekeeper and told him, 'Three days ago my donkey died, and I have nothing to plow with.' My grandfather refused to give in, and the peasant had to return the queen bee. On the way home the beekeeper saw that the bee had a sore on her throat just where the yoke had rubbed her neck. He tried his best to heal her with all kinds of remedies, but they did not help. At last he took a nut, ground it into powder, and rubbed it on the wound. Afterward he lay under a tree and fell asleep. When he woke up, he could not believe his eyes. By the side of the tree under which he had been sleeping, another nut tree had sprung up. He understood that the tree had grown from the powder he had put on the queen bee's sore. A colossal nut was hanging on the tree, and he wanted to pick it. He took a clod of earth and threw it away above. Suddenly a field appeared over the tree, and in the field wheat began to grow under the very eyes of my grandfather. At that moment a boar appeared. My grandfather got hold of him, tied a scythe to his tail, and threw him up above into the field. While running in the field, the boar cut the wheat with the scythe. My grandfather collected the wheat and brought it to the miller. The miller ground it and baked the bread. Then the old man took it home."

When the merchant's son uttered the words "took it home," he grabbed hold of the big loaf of bread and ran home with it.

Part III
Talking Animals

·25· Abraham Our Father and the Dogs

IFA 1230. Told by Shoshana Goldenberg, as heard in her youth in Lithuania.

A variation on Type 930*, Fate Foretold as Punishment, including Motif B217, "Animal language learned." For Middle East analogues, see H. Schwarzbaum, "The Jewish and Moslem Versions of Some Theodicy Legends," Fabula, III (1959), 164, Note 222; and I. Olsvanger, Raisins with Almonds (Rosinkes mit Mandeln) (Basel, 1921), No. 366, and L'Chayim! (the Hebrew toast) (New York, 1949), No. 174. Type 930* is reported from Lithuania, Denmark, and Greece. It is a subform of Type 930, The Prophecy, a widely distributed tale that is well known in eastern Europe.

• An old Jew once met another old man of a fine countenance with twinkling eyes. The stranger revealed that he was none other than Abraham our Father and added, "Ask a boon, and it will be granted."

The Jew requested that the old man teach him the language of animals. Abraham our Father fulfilled this request, and the Jew was able to understand what domestic animals were saying among themselves, as well as the language of birds and flies.

Once the old Jew was listening to his dogs barking, and he heard them say, "Today we will have good food because the cow, here, will die."

Immediately, the Jew took his cow to the market and sold it to a peasant.

The next day he again listened to the dogs barking. "Today we shall have good food because a fire will break out here and the master will be too busy to watch us and we shall be able to eat up everything in the house and the cellar."

With great speed the Jew sold his house and removed all his possessions.

On the third day he again heard his dogs barking. "Today a

great disaster will take place at our master's house. His wife will die."

The old Jew began to weep. What should he do? He went to the rabbi and told him all that had taken place: how Abraham our Father had taught him the language of animals so he could understand his dogs, how he had sold his cow and his home, and how he had been told by his dogs that his wife would die today. What should he do to save her?

The rabbi said to him, "You stupid Jew! Abraham our Father had your welfare in mind, but you misunderstood him. He intended your cows and house to be sacrificed in place of your wife, but as you sold them, you prevented this. Now your wife will not be able to recover, and it is not in your power to save her from death."

•26• *The Span of Man's Life*

IFA 256. Recorded by Sara Fishbein, housewife, from her father, Kathriel Schwarz, who heard the story from his grandfather in Galicia, Poland.

A version of Type 828, Men and Animals Readjust Span of Life, *and Motifs A1321,* "Men and animals readjust span of life," *and B592,* "Animals bequeath characteristics to man." *In most of the versions the man reaches seventy years only. Cf. Ps. 90:10,* "The days of our years are three score years and ten." *This tale is reported from India, Lithuania, and Hungary, and is in Grimms' collection, No. 176,* "The Span of Life."

• WHEN THE Holy One created Adam, he showed him the beauty of the world and said, "You will rule over all you see, and you will be very happy."

"How long will I be able to enjoy all this goodness?" enquired Adam.

"Thirty years," was the answer.

"Such a short time?" asked Adam in surprise. "Could you not add a few extra years?"

The Holy One, blessed be he, meditated and answered, "I shall call a few animals. Maybe they will be prepared to grant you some extra years of life as a gift."

The first to appear was the donkey. Said the Holy One, blessed be he, "Your fate is to work hard, to carry burdens, and to eat a little grass in your master's courtyard."

"How many years will I live?" asked the donkey.

"Forty," came the answer.

"Why must I suffer for so many years?" brayed the donkey in a sad voice. "I shall be satisfied with half that time—twenty years."

The Holy One, blessed be he, gave the extra twenty years to Adam, who was radiant with joy and happiness: with this gift he would live for fifty years.

Then the Holy One, blessed be he, spoke to the dog, "Your fate is to be a faithful friend of your master and to guard him and his property. Your reward will be to eat scraps of food and receive blows and kicks."

"How many years will I live?" asked the dog.

"Forty," came the answer.

"Why should I suffer for so many years?" barked the dog in a sad voice. "Half that time, twenty years, is enough for me."

So the Holy One, blessed be he, took twenty years from the dog's life and added them to the life of Adam, who was radiant with joy and happiness: with this gift he would live for seventy years.

The Holy One, blessed be he, then spoke to the monkey saying, "Your fate is to walk on two feet and to make men laugh at your gait, for it is very queer to him. As for food, you will be thrown scraps from time to time."

"How many years will I live?" asked the monkey.

"Sixty years," was the answer.

"Why so long? Half that time is enough for me."

So the Holy One, blessed be he, took the thirty years from the monkey's life and gave them as a gift to Adam, who was radiant with joy and happiness because he would live an extra thirty years. Since that time the life span of man has been one hundred years divided into four periods.

The first period is until the age of thirty, when a man enjoys the years of his own life to the full and is strong, independent, and carefree.

In the second period, from thirty to fifty years, he is usually married and a father. He has the burden of earning a living and providing for his family. To satisfy his children's and wife's needs, he works like a donkey. These are the twenty years of a donkey's life.

In the third period, from fifty to seventy years, a man serves his children and guards their property as a faithful dog. Usually he does not eat at his children's table. These are the twenty years of a dog's life.

Then comes the last period, from the age of seventy to one hundred. In that period, man loses his teeth, his face becomes wrinkled, and his way of walking and his movements are strange. His children laugh and make fun of him, and it is as if he had departed from this life. These are the thirty years of a monkey's life.

·27· *The Cat's Allotment*

IFA 196. Recorded by Nachum Raphael, born in Libya, as he heard it in his youth. Cf. Motif A2435.3.2, "Food of cat."

• WHEN THE Almighty allotted the means of living, he asked the cat, "From whom do you want to receive your daily bread: the shopkeeper, the peasant, or the peddlar?"

The cat answered wholeheartedly, "Give me my daily bread from an absent-minded woman who leaves the kitchen door open."

·28· *Till I Prove Who I Am*

IFA 581. Recorded by Shalom Dervish, a lawyer, who heard the tale in Iraq in his youth.

For a variant of this joke, see A. Druyanov, The Book of Jokes and Wit, Vol. II, No. 1946. In his notes, p. 458, he cites still another version (a rabbit instead of a fox) that was circulating in Russia at the time of the revolution of 1905 and had a political coloring.

• THERE IS A saying among Babylonian (Iraqi) Jews in their Arabic dialect: "Till you prove who I am, there is time enough to strip off my skin."

Here is the story upon which this saying is based.

Once a fox was seen running away. He was asked, "Why are you running away?"

He answered, "Hunters are chasing camels, killing them, and stripping off their skins."

The people were amazed. "But you are a fox not a camel, are you not?"

The fox answered, "Till I prove who I am, there is time enough to strip off my skin."

•29• *How a Dove and a Snake Took Pity on a Man*

IFA 1845. Recorded by Heda Jason from Jefet Shvili, a Yemen-born laborer, who heard the story from a fellow worker born in Iraq.

Type 160, Grateful Animals: Ungrateful Man. For Jewish versions of this tale, see N. Gross, pp. 257–59; A. S. Rappoport, Folklore of the Jews, p. 141–44; and M. J. Bin Gorion, Der Born Judas, IV, 51–57, 277. For Turkish texts, see W. Eberhard-P. N. Boratav, No. 65, "Der Dank von Taube und Schlange." Arabic literary treatments of this type are listed in V. Chauvin, Vol. II, p. 106, No. 71. A medieval European literary example is in the Gesta Romanorum, *No. 119. The tale is reported from India and Africa as well as from many European countries. A recently published text from Dagestan can be found in N. Kapieva, Dagestan Folktales, No. 13.*

• THERE WAS ONCE a rich man. He was aged, and before he died he entreated his son, "Have mercy on animals but not on men." Then he breathed his last.

The son remained alone. Once when he was wandering in a field, he saw a dove. The dove was whimpering, as one of her wings was broken. The man took her out of the thicket, gave her food and drink, and brought her home. He put her in a cage and sent for a doctor.

On his arrival the doctor asked, "Well, where is the sick man?"

The son brought the cage.

"What is it?"

"Here is the sick one."

"Are you mad? Are you prepared to pay for it."

"Yes, as much as you want."

"Pay ten pounds down."

The son paid the money, whereupon the doctor examined the dove. He gave her an injection and medicine and said, "Leave her, and tomorrow I shall come to see her again, but I shall not ask for more money."

The dove was under treatment for several days and then recovered.

Another time the son was in the field and saw a snake. The poor snake had been given a blow on the neck and was lying ill. The ants had already begun to nibble at him. The son took pity on the snake and put a handkerchief alongside it. The snake crawled on to the handkerchief, and the son picked it up and took it home. Then he ran to the doctor.

"Again? What is the matter?" said the doctor in surprise. "Where are the sick birds?"

"There are no sick birds today. I have a snake this time. Don't be afraid," he said to the doctor. "I will hold it and you examine it."

"First pay."

"Here is ten pounds." The doctor examined the snake, applied ointment, and gave it pills, whereupon the snake recovered.

It so happened that at this time there was a man in the country who had committed a crime. He had stolen something or committed some offence. Whatever it may have been, he was taken outside and stoned. However he remained alive, and the stones missed his head.

The son was walking one day when lo! he heard groans. "Aa, Aa, Aa, Aa." Approaching, he saw a man who had been stoned, yet was still alive. Now it was known that if a man was stoned, yet remained alive, he was to be set free and was not punished again.

The son said to himself, "My father told me to have pity on animals and not on men, but he was not right. Here is a man who has remained alive after being stoned. It seems that he was not guilty, and I shall save him." Approaching the man, he took him out from under the heap of stones and went to call for the doctor. The doctor came and took double payment because this time it was a man who was sick.

When the man recovered, he said to his rescuer, "Look, I am lonely. I have no wife and no brother; in fact, I have nobody in the whole world. Let us be brothers. I have here six cases of gold, and they will be yours and mine. If I die they will all be yours, and if you die they will all be mine." They both agreed.

One day a case of gold was stolen from the king. It was proclaimed, "Whoever finds the case of gold and the thief will become vizier."

The man who was stoned and saved from death said to himself, "I shall go and tell that my brother is the thief. They will take one case and stone him, and the rest will be mine." And so it was. He ran off and accused the other.

The king asked, "How did you get hold of him?" The man answered, "No matter. What is important is that he is the thief."

Then the king asked him, "Didn't we stone you a short time ago?"

"Yes, that is right, but I was not killed. Men on camels came and saved me. I went with them, and I took what they had and went off."

The soldiers went and brought the case which the man had put aside from the others. The king did not examine it to see if it was the same case that was stolen, and the man was appointed vizier.

As for the man who saved him, a trap was laid for him on his way back from work.

When they caught him, he shouted, "What have I done?"

"What have you done, you dare to shout? You stole the case!"

The man understood that his "brother" had turned him over. As he was taken off to be stoned, he said to himself, "Alas! my father was right; one shouldn't take pity on men." However, he too did not die when he was stoned but struggled between life and death.

In the house the dove and the snake awaited him, and they were very surprised when he did not come to feed them. Meanwhile they had become friendly and had reached an understanding.

"What has happened?" the snake asked the dove.

"How do I know? Fly down over the town, and search for him." The dove flew over the town till she found him. She flew down and perched near him. The man indicated with his finger that he was thirsty. The dove flew away and came back with water. She flew again and again until he had drunk enough. She also brought him food and fed him. Then she flew home and recounted everything to the snake.

"What can we do?" the snake said. "Take me on your wing." They flew together to their deliverer. They decided that the snake with its poisonous mouth should not feed the man, and so the dove would care for him while the snake found a way to save him. The snake went to the king's palace and kept his daughter in a tight grip by winding himself around her stomach. The daughter cried out in great pain. The doctors came, but none of them could drag the snake away. As they tried to approach the snake immediately began to hiss, and no one knew what to do. The daughter was nearing death because she was unable to eat.

The king said, "Whoever saves my daughter will become king in my place."

In the meantime passers-by saw the man who had been stoned.

"Are you alive?" they asked in surprise.

"Yes. What is going on in town?"

"The king's daughter is ill. A snake has caught hold of her, and no one knows how to shake him off."

"Go to the king and tell him that I will get rid of the snake." They informed the king, and he said, "Bring him here; it seems that he was not guilty because he has survived." The man was picked up, washed and dressed, and brought to the snake, who was hissing and would not allow anyone to approach.

The man came and laid down a handkerchief. The snake quietly unwound itself from the daughter and crawled onto the handkerchief, which the man then put in his pocket.

The king was surprised and said, "How did you do this?"

"It's nothing, my king. May I go home? I have enough money and do not need anything from you."

"On your life! Explain how you did it." The king would not let the man go until he had told him everything. At last the man said, "My king, you have not examined the case of gold. Come and see that I have five more cases at home exactly the same. And there is also a dove there."

The king went to the house and found that everything was as the man had said. Immediately, the king called his new vizier. When the vizier saw his so-called brother, he became frightened.

"He is right. I beg your pardon for what I have done," the vizier said.

"So this is what you are," shouted the king angrily. "This man saved your life, and you, ungrateful creature, betrayed him!"

The vizier was stoned, and indeed, this time he died.

Part IV
Kings and Commoners

IFA 412. Recorded by Zvulun Kort, as heard in Afghanistan in his youth.

Type 1736A, Sword Turns to Wood. The hero humorously takes advantage of the belief expressed in Motif H215.1, "Sword magically changed to wood when executioner is to decapitate innocent person." The tale contains as well Motifs K1812.1, "Incognito king helped by humble man," and Q45, "Hospitality rewarded." The optimistic phrase used by the hero is a biblical quotation from Psalms 68:20. Four Turkish versions of this type are cited in W. Eberhard-P N. Boratav, No. 309, "Der Zufriedene." It is also reported from Greece, Finland, Germany, Czechoslovakia, and Italy. A Sephardic Jewish text is given in A. D. L. Palacin, No. 127, and an Uzbek example is given in M. I. Shewerdin, Vol. II, Nos. 132, 137.

· SHAH ABBAS, the king, liked justice and righteousness. Evening after evening he used to disguise himself and roam around the streets of the town in order to get to know more about his subjects. Generally, he used to disguise himself as a dervish (Moslem monk) and go to the outskirts of the town, to share the life of the needy.

Once, on his usual route, he was struck by a dim light. When he came nearer he saw a humble cottage. A man was sitting inside, in front of his meal, singing songs and benedictions. Shah Abbas entered and asked, "Is a guest welcome here?"

"A guest is the Lord's gift, sir. Sit down, please, and join me," the answer came.

Shah Abbas sat down, and the man entertained him freely. They talked about this and that. Asked Shah Abbas, "What is your trade? What do you do for a living?"

Replied the man, "I am a cobbler. During the day, I wander around the town mending people's shoes. With the pennies I earn, I buy food in the evening."

Asked Shah Abbas, "And what of tomorrow?"

Answered the shoemaker, "Blessed be God, day by day."

Shah Abbas went on sitting with the man and enjoyed the conversation. Then he parted from him, saying, "Tomorrow I will come again."

Shah Abbas returned home, and the next morning he put up a proclamation in the streets of the town prohibiting the repair of shoes without a permit. When Shah Abbas came the next evening to visit the cobbler, he found him eating, drinking, and enjoying life as before.

He asked him, "What have you done today?"

"On leaving home, I heard the Shah's herald proclaiming that the repair of shoes was prohibited. I went on my way and started to draw water for some of the citizens. Thus I earned my daily bread."

"I worried about you very much," said Shah Abbas, "when I heard that mending shoes was forbidden. Now what will you do if the king forbids drawing water?"

The cobbler answered, "Blessed be God, day by day."

Shah Abbas went home, and the following morning he prohibited the drawing of water. When Shah Abbas came the next evening to visit the cobbler, he found him eating, drinking, and enjoying life as before. He greeted him and asked, "What have you done today?"

The cobbler told him, "I chopped wood and thus earned my daily bread."

Shah Abbas asked, "And what if tomorrow the chopping of wood is forbidden?"

"Blessed be God, day by day," answered the cobbler. They both sat together as usual and passed the time pleasantly. On parting the disguised king promised to come the next evening.

Early the following morning the Shah's herald proclaimed that all woodchoppers were to be recruited into the king's guard. The cobbler went to the palace and was given a sword and sent on guard. Evening came, and he went to a shop and pledged his sword blade to the shopkeeper. Then he bought his usual food and went home. There he took a piece of wood, made a wooden blade, attached it to his sword hilt, and put it into his sheath.

In the evening the disguised king came again to the humble

cottage and asked "What is new? What have you done today?"

The man told him, "I was on guard in the palace, and I did not earn any money. So I gave my sword blade as a pledge to the shopkeeper and bought my usual food. Now I have made a wooden blade."

The king asked, "What will happen if there is a sword inspection tomorrow?"

The man answered, "Blessed be God, day by day."

Next morning, the officer in charge of the palace guard called the cobbler and handed over a prisoner to him, saying, "This prisoner has been sentenced to death, and you are ordered to behead him."

Pleaded the cobbler, "I have never in my life killed a man! I cannot do so."

The officer-in-charge commanded, "Do as you have been told!"

The man clasped the hilt of his sword in one hand and grasped the sheath in the other. Then he proclaimed before the people assembled for the execution: "Almighty One in Heaven! It is known to you that I am not a murderer. If this prisoner is marked for death, let my sword be of steel, but if the prisoner is innocent, let the steel blade turn into wood." And saying this, he pulled out the blade. And lo! It was wood. The assembled crowd watched in silent amazement.

Then Shah Abbas called the cobbler, embraced and kissed him, revealed his identity, and appointed him as one of the court advisors.

• 31 • The Peasant Who Learned To Like Coffee

IFA 14. Recorded by Elisheva Schoenfeld in Affula in 1956 from Mordechai "Marko" Litsi, born in Turkey.

On coffee as a subject in Arab folktales, see E. Littmann, Arabische Märchen . . . , p. 448, s.v. "Koffee." Motifs present in the story are P14.19, "King goes in disguise at night to observe his subjects" (*cf. Nos. 32 and 35, in this book, IFA 1185 and IFA 1919*), *K1812.4, "Incognito king is given hospitality by fisherman," Q111.2, "Riches as reward (for hospitality)," and L113, "Hero of unpromising occupation." These are common to many folktales in the eastern Mediterranean, but the twist, in which the peasant praises coffee after complaining about the king's high taxes, is unusual.*

• MANY YEARS AGO the sultan decided to wander across the country in disguise with his vizier and see with his own eyes how his people really lived. On the first day they reached a small peasant's cottage. It was noon, and they were thirsty. They knocked at the door and asked for a cup of water. The peasant invited them to come in and share his meal. They accepted his hospitality and seated themselves on the floor. Meanwhile the peasant went into his garden and brought back a pomegranate. He squeezed out the juice, and just this one fruit was enough to fill a big cup to the brim. The peasant handed it to his guests who drank the juice in a gulp.

"This drink is delicious!" exclaimed the sultan. And he said within his heart, "I am a king, and yet I do not have such tasty drinks in my cellars."

At the end of the meal, the sultan and his vizier thanked the peasant for his kindness and continued their journey.

Some months passed, and once more the two travelers arrived at the same cottage. This time, too, the peasant went into his garden to bring pomegranates. He squeezed the fruit, but alas! the juice did not fill even a quarter of the cup. The peasant needed three more fruits to fill it. The sultan drank the juice, but the taste was quite different this time.

"What is the matter?" the sultan asked. "Do you not have more of the delicious pomegranates which we tasted on our first visit?"

"Unfortunately not," answered the peasant. "The pomegranates are no longer as good as they were, and I have become poor." He began to curse the sultan, who demanded such high taxes that nothing remained for the peasants.

Hearing the peasant's complaints and curses, the sultan wrote a few words on a piece of paper and handed it to the peasant, saying, "If you make up your mind to come to the city, here is my address. I shall help you to find work. Seeing this note, everyone will be able to tell you where I live."

The peasant put the message into his pocket and thanked his guests.

Some time passed. There was no work for the peasant, and conditions were getting worse and worse. So he sold all his possessions and left for the city to search for work. Suddenly he remembered the message of his two guests. He showed it to a policeman he met on the way, who was astonished when he recognized the signature of the sultan himself. Of course he did not say a word to the peasant but sent him to the sultan's palace. When the peasant arrived there and tried to enter at the main gate, the watchman stopped him.

The sultan, seeing something strange going on at the gate, looked out through the window and saw the peasant standing there. He immediately ordered the watchman to let him in. Then the peasant realized that his guest had been no other than the sultan himself.

When the peasant appeared before him, the sultan greeted him and said, "If you are looking for work, I am ready to take you on as a gardener. And if you are a good worker, I shall increase your pay."

The peasant was only too pleased to accept this offer. Before he set out to work, the king invited him to drink a cup of coffee. The peasant was not familiar with this drink and burnt his lips.

A year passed, and by this time the peasant had learned to read and write. One day the king called him and said, "You have worked well. I am prepared to appoint you as a tax inspector in the harbor. Your work will be to write down whatever goods enter and leave the country. Every night you will have to bring me a written report."

The peasant began working at the harbor and carried out his job honestly.

One day a ship, loaded with coffee, reached the port, but the tax inspector did not let it enter. The same happened every time a ship came in with coffee. Soon the price of coffee went up. The coffee merchants became so worried that they went to the sultan and told him that the new tax inspector turned away all shipments of coffee.

The sultan called for the peasant and gave him a cup of coffee, the most beloved drink of the Turks. He said to him, "Do not drink it all at once but sip by sip."

Slowly the peasant drank the coffee and enjoyed its fragrant taste. At last he understood that coffee was a most delicious drink.

Since that time he was always very happy when a shipment of coffee arrived in the harbor.

·*32*· *When I Lift the Left Moustache*

IFA 1185. Recorded by Zvulun Kort, as heard in his youth in Afghanistan.

A version of Type 951A*, Three Thieves Rob the Treasury. Cf. Motifs P14.19, "King goes in disguise at night to observe his subjects" (also in Nos. 31 and 35 in this book), and K1812.2, "Incognito king joins robbers." References to this motif in Oriental folktales are found in N. M. Penzer (ed.), The Ocean of Story, II, 183, n. 1; and VII, 215. M. Bloomfield discusses this motif, among others, in his article "The Art of Stealing in Hindu Fiction," American Journal of Philology, *XLIV (1923), 193–229. A text from central Asia is given in M. I. Shewerdin, Vol II, No. 142, and a variant among the Sephardic Jews is given in M. Grunwald, No. 29. The fraternal relationship between a prince and outlaws is one of the central themes in Shakespeare's* Henry IV; *Lord Raglan comments on its folkloristic significance in* The Hero *(3d ed.; New York: Evergreen Books, 1956), pp. 206–16.*

· SHAH ABBAS was a king who loved justice and righteousness. Evening after evening he used to leave his palace and wander in disguise on the outskirts of the town so as to observe the life of the poor people.

One evening he went to the outskirts and saw a dim light in the distance. He set out in that direction and came to a humble hut. He entered and saw three people sitting round a smouldering fire, smoking a *nargila*. He said, "Good evening!" and asked, "Is a guest welcome?"

"A guest is a gift of God. Sit down with us, please," came the answer. They spoke about this and that, and the king asked, "What is your trade? How do you make a living?"

The first answered, "I know the language of animals." The second answered, "If I see a man once, even in the dark, I always recognize him." The third answered, "I have a key that opens every latch and door."

"And how do you make a living?" they asked the king.

"By lifting the right moustache I build the world, and by lifting the left one I ruin the world."

"What scheme have you in mind at present?" the king asked them.

"This evening we are going to break into the state treasury and snatch the valuables," came the answer. The four men set off on their way. After a short while they came across a dog. He began to bark, and another dog joined in. They asked the first man, "Why were the dogs barking?"

He answered, "The first dog said, 'Thieves are coming.' His friend answered 'Do not worry, the boss is with them.'"

They continued on their way in darkness, led by the second man, until they reached the treasury. The third man opened a side door; whereupon they went inside and took some valuable possessions, including diamonds, pearls, and other jewels. Then they came out and shut the door as if nothing had happened. No one noticed their movements. They divided the spoils, and each one went on his way. The king returned, of course, to his palace.

Early in the morning the king sat on his throne with a red cap on his head, as a sign of anger. He summoned all his ministers. On seeing the red cap on his head, a deep fear filled their hearts. The king approached the minister of the treasury and ordered him to bring a certain precious pearl from the treasury. The minister ran to bring the pearl. He entered the treasury—and what a calamity! The pearl was not there.

He looked here and there and noticed that many valuables were missing. He examined the doors and saw they were intact. With unsteady steps he returned to the king, fell on his knees, and said, "My lord and king! The pearl is not there, and I do not know who took it away."

The king was enraged and called out, "If you are the minister of the treasury, how is it you do not know what is going on? I will grant you three days, and if you do not find the missing jewels, you will be beheaded."

The minister of the treasury made inquiries all over town but found no clue. On the third day the king sent police to the hut of his three friends, and they were brought before him. They fell on their faces and bowed their heads in shame. The police lifted them up. Shah Abbas made believe that he was angry with them and began questioning them, "What do you do? How do you make a living?"

There was no answer. "You are guilty of breaking into the king's treasury. I sentence you to death!" The king lifted his left moustache and ordered the chief slaughterer, "Unsheath your sword!"

At that moment the second accomplice opened his mouth and said, "Long live the king! Now it is time for you to lift the right moustache. I am the man who having once seen a person, even in the dark, recognizes him always."

The king understood the allusion, smiled, and revoked the decree, "Put back your sword into its sheath." And in appreciation of their courage, he appointed the three friends as his bodyguards.

· 33 ·   A Brother's Love

IFA 1963. Recorded by Ya'aḳov Avitsuḳ, a farmer from Meir Ezra, born in Persian Kurdistan.

Type 950, Rhampsinitus, a celebrated tale written down by Herodotus in the fifth century B.C. and carried by oral tradition from India to Iceland. Over two hundred texts have been collected in Ireland, and it is known to Caucasian, Turḳestan, and Berber storytellers. When Stith Thompson discussed Rhampsinitus in 1946 (The Folktale, pp. 171–72), he commented that in the New World it had been reported only from Cape Verde Islanders in Massachusetts. However, in his 1961 revision of the Type-Index, he was able to locate thirty-one texts in South, Central, and North America, in French, Spanish, and Negro traditions.

Jewish versions from eastern Europe are given in Y. L. Cahan Yiddishe Folksmayses *(1931), Nos. 20 and 31 (reprinted in Cahan [1940], Nos. 31 and 42), and are discussed by Beatrice S. Weinreich in "Four Variants of the Yiddish Master Thief Tale," The Field of Yiddish, ed. Uriel Weinreich (New York, 1954), pp. 199–213. Arab literary versions are noted in V. Chauvin, VIII, 185–86.*

THERE WERE two brothers who lived with their mother. The elder brother had no wife; the younger one was married and had three children. The two brothers had no work, and so they decided to rob the king's treasury. They succeeded in stealing a bag full of gold, although forty-five soldiers were on guard.

On the next day the king found out that thieves had stolen from his treasury without having been caught or disturbed by the watchmen. The king sent messengers to an old man who was very clever and invited him to the palace. When the old man came, the king said to him, "Advise me, please, how to catch the thieves."

The old man heard the king's words and said, "We shall bring to the palace a barrel full of pitch, and we shall use it to cover the floor of the treasury." And so they did. Afterward they put bundles of straw on the floor and set them afire. The smoke went out through a hole in the wall, and so they knew how the thieves had broken into the treasury. However, the counselor told the king, "Who the thieves were, I do not know."

The day passed, and in the darkness of the night both the brothers again made their way to the treasury. The elder brother entered first and sank into the pitch. He whispered to his brother, "Look, I am sinking into the pitch. It reaches already to my shoulders. Take your sword and cut my head off! Then take it with you. Thus your wife and children will be able to survive. Otherwise they will identify me and kill all of you."

The younger brother cut off his brother's head and returned home. Next day the watchmen discovered a man's body in the pitch, and so they knew that he was the thief. But when they attempted to identify the body, they could not do it, as it was headless.

The king again gave orders to call his old counselor and told him, "All your counsels have proved successful. Indeed, the thief came again, and he sank into the pitch. We cannot, however, identify him, as his head is missing. Please tell me how to identify the body. If you succeed again, you will receive a great reward."

The counselor answered, "My lord and king! We have in our courtyard a bird which we free whenever a king dies. It then sits on the head of the future king. I suggest we now free this bird. Let it fly where it likes. The roof of the house where the bird will rest is the home of the thief." The king accepted the counsel and ordered the bird set free. And the bird flew straight to the house of the younger brother—the thief.

But even before the counselor gave his advice to the king, the younger brother had bought a bow and arrows. And one day, when he saw a beautiful bird on the roof of his house, he shot and killed it. He ran toward the bird, brought it home, and warned his mother, "Hide the bird in a place where nobody can ever find it."

That day a woman came to the king. "Give me money, please," she addressed him, "and I shall reveal to you who the thief is."

The king agreed. The woman had for a long time suspected the younger brother, as he was a hunter, and so might have been a thief too. She went to visit him, entered his home in his absence, and approached the mother. "Have you any bird meat? My son is very sick, and only the meat of a bird can save him."

The hunter's mother was moved and agreed to give a piece of the bird to her visitor. At that moment, however, the son returned from the hunt. When he saw the woman with a piece of meat in her hand, he called her back. "I shall give you some more meat, as my hunt was very successful today."

The woman returned, but when she entered the house, he caught her and cut her tongue off. The woman shouted and cried as her pains were excruciating, and when she left, her hands were red with blood. She made a bloody sign on the door of the hunter's house and departed for the king's palace. There she started to stutter, but it was enough for the king to send messengers to look for the bloodstained house of the thief.

In the meantime the thief stained all the other houses with

blood, and the king's servants found bloodstained doors at all the houses. There was no possiblility at all of distinguishing the thief's door from any other one.

The king again called the old counselor. He advised the king to wash the dead body and to put it at the crossroads: "We can be sure that the members of the family will come to mourn and to weep on the body."

And, indeed, so it was done. What, however, did the younger brother do? He told his mother, "Go to the market place and buy a few glasses there. Then pass with them near the dead body. I shall come riding on a horse, push you, and break your glasses. Then you will weep, but nobody will suspect you of mourning at the thief's body."

The mother bought glasses, and while passing the crossroads, a rider pushed her, and all her glasses broke. She wept bitterly. Immediately the king's watchmen caught her and brought her before the king. He accused her, "You wept over your son's body!"

The mother argued, "You are wrong, my lord and king. I spent much money for the glasses, and here they are, all of them broken by a cruel rider. How can I abstain from weeping?"

The watchmen confirmed the woman's story. The king gave her money to buy new glasses and freed her.

A few days passed, and a bad smell of the unburied body filled the town. The citizens could not stand this smell and asked the king to bury the body, as none of the thief's relatives had come to mourn for him.

The king gave orders to bury the body, and the thief has not been found until this very day.

· 34 · He Who Gives Thanks to the King and He Who Gives Thanks to the Almighty

IFA 458. Recorded by Zvulun Kort, as heard from the late Rabbi Joseph Gurgji, chief rabbi of the Afghanistan Jews in Jerusalem.

Type 841, One Beggar Trusts God, the Other the King. *IFA versions of this type originated in Yemen, Afghanistan, Bukhara, Russia, and Iraq; for another variant, see No. 67, (in this book), "The Tailor with His Luck Locked Up" (IFA 8) and the head-note. Palestinian-Arab texts are given in Abu Naaman, No. 27, and J. E. Hanauer, pp, 162–64.*

• Two BEGGARS used to wander in the streets day by day collecting alms. On their way they used to pass the king's palace, and he always gave them charity. One of the beggars always praised the king for his goodness and generosity. The other one used to thank God that he was generous to the king and enabled him to help his subjects. This was painful to the king, and once he said to the beggar, "It is I who am generous to you, and you offer thanks to someone else."

The beggar answered, "If God were not bountiful, you would not be able to give."

One day the king ordered his baker to bake two similar loaves of bread and to put precious stones in only one of them as a gift from the king. Then he ordered that the loaf with the jewels be given to the beggar who praised the king and the ordinary loaf to the other beggar.

The baker took care not to mix up the two loaves. He handed the one with the treasure to the beggar who praised the king and the ordinary one to the beggar who praised God.

When the two beggars left the palace, the beggar who praised the king observed that his loaf was heavy and seemed to be badly baked. He asked his friend to exchange loaves with him. His friend, wanting to do a good turn, agreed; whereupon they parted, each going his own way.

The beggar who praised God began to eat, and of course he found the treasure in the bread. He offered thanks to God that he would not have to go to the palace each day and stretch out his hand for alms.

The king was very surprised that this beggar no longer came, and he asked the baker, "Did you not make a mistake when you handed over the two loaves of bread to the two beggars?"

The baker answered, "I did exactly as you ordered, my king!"

The king asked the beggar, "What did you do with the loaf of bread that was given to you the other day?"

Replied the beggar, "The loaf was hard, and it did not seem to be well baked; so I exchanged it with my fellow beggar."

Now the king understood that riches come from God alone. Only He can turn a rich man into a poor man and a poor man into a rich man. The decision and the will of a man, be he even a king, may not be realized.

· 35 ·　*A Letter to the Almighty*

IFA 1919. Recorded by Meir Amrusi from his Tunisian-born father.

For another Jewish version of this tale in which Rothschild replaces the king, see A. Druyanov, Vol. III, No. 2088, and N. Gross, pp. 283–84. Usually Motif J2461.1, "Literal following of instructions about action," has a humorous consequence. Cf. Types 1692, Stupid Thief, and 1693, The Literal Fool. However, because of the economic situation of the hero, this humorous effect is missing here, and the tale ends with Motif Q45, "Hospitality rewarded." For a discussion of the actual practice of believers' sending letters to heaven or to saints, see Walter Heim, Breif zum Himmel (Basel, 1961).

Motif P14.19, "King goes in disguise at night to observe his subjects," has also appeared in Nos. 31 and 32 in this book (IFA 14 and 1185).

· THERE WERE once two brothers. One was rich, and the other was poor. The poor brother was supported by the rich one, who was the elder. Every Thursday evening he used to go to the home of the rich brother to receive something, hardly enough to last the week.

One day the rich brother had to travel to a distant town. His journey would take a month to get there and a month to come back. The poor brother, miserable one that he was, went as usual to his brother's home. The first week his sister-in-law supported him as usual. The second and third weeks she sent him away and advised him, "Ask the Almighty."

As soon as the poor brother heard the advice, he went at once to write a letter. And this is what he wrote:

"In honor of the Holy One, blessed be he. Do you know that Passover draws near, and I need much money because I have a number of expenses? I beg you to send me, by return, enough money to suffice for Passover. With thanks."

The man put the letter in an envelope and wrote on it, "To the Holy One, Blessed Be He in Heaven." He waited for a wind. At last a wind came and blew the letter, bringing it right to the king's palace in a distant city.

The king found the letter within his castle, picked it up, and opened it. He saw it was written in Hebrew, and as he could not understand the language, he called the rabbi and showed him the letter. The rabbi translated it for the king.

"The Almighty sent me this letter," said the king, "so I must send this man all he needs."

He at once gave an order to one of his servants to load two camels with choice supplies: two lambs, a bag of gold, and a bundle of silver. "Follow the camels," said the king, "and see where they lead you."

The servant did as the king bade him. He followed the camels till at last they reached the poor man's house. When the poor man saw the two camels outside, he was overjoyed, believing that the Holy One, blessed be he, had sent all this. He immediately set about repairing his house and painting it. Yet he still had money left over.

In due time the rich brother returned from his journey and asked his wife, "Did you give my brother his allowance as usual each week?"

"Just the first week," came the answer.

"And the rest of the time?"

"I told him to ask the Almighty for the rest."

The rich man was very grieved at these tidings. What can a man do when he has such a bad wife?

He had a bit of food and then quickly set off to his brother's house. At last he arrived there, and lo! he did not recognize it.

In place of a hut stood a beautiful house. The rich man knocked at the door; whereupon his brother opened it and related the whole story.

The rich brother was very happy, and the younger brother asked him to celebrate Passover at his house. And so it was agreed to hold the Seder there together.

On the Seder evening, the rich man's wife saw a gold cup on the table with the king's name on it. The next day she wrote a letter to the king, accusing her brother-in-law of theft. The king received the letter and straight away he came to the town, dressed in ordinary clothes, and went to the younger brother's house.

The younger brother was delighted with his guest and treated him well. Not recognizing the king, the host said, "You look like an honest man; so I should like to be your friend. To remember this visit and as a sign of friendship, I want to give you a cup that I received as a gift from the Almighty."

The king was delighted by the reception and by his host's generosity and answered, "Many thanks. Take it to the jeweler, and I shall pay you its worth."

As the cup was studded with precious stones, the king paid one thousand pounds for it.

Afterward the king gave orders to his servants to bring the man's rich brother and his wife before him. Thereupon he asked the rich man, "Have you children from this wife?"

"I have," said the man.

The king gave orders to kill the rich man's evil and jealous wife.

The rich man married again, and the couple lived a good and happy life.

And the brother? He no longer needed help and lived in happiness and wealth. Would that this was so with all of us.

Part V
Clever Jews

· 36 · A Judge of Horses, Diamonds, and Men

IFA 327. Recorded by Nehama Zion, a housewife, from her Hungarian-born grandfather.

This tale revolves around the general Motif J1661.1, "Deduction from observation." The specific Motif J1661.1.2, "Deduction: king is a bastard," appears in Type 655, The Wise Brothers along with other clever deductions. An east European-Jewish text can be found in Gross, pp. 229–32. Type 655 appears throughout Europe and in India, Indonesia, Africa, and Arab countries. Jewish literary versions are in M. Gaster, Exempla of the Rabbis, Nos. 51, 83, 372, and Gaster (ed.), Ma'aseh Book, No. 155. Three texts from Uzbekistan are printed by M. I. Shewerdin, Vol. I, No. 23, and Vol. II, Nos. 127, 151; one from the Caucasus is given in S. Britajev-K. Kasbekov, No. 19; and one from Kazakhstan is given in W. Sidelnikov, No. 41.

• IN ONE OF the towns of the Diaspora, there lived a Jew who was a judge of horses, jewelry, and men, and he made his livelihood through this ability.

It so happened that the king in the nearby capital was shown a large diamond necklace which he wanted to give as a gift to his wife, the queen. The king sent for the Jew, who appeared at the king's palace, examined the necklace, and then gave his opinion: "The diamonds are false and have no value, not even one thousandth of the price that is demanded."

The king was pleased he had saved money, and gave the Jew a petty coin. The Jew thanked the king and returned home.

After a short time, the king wanted to add a fine horse to his stock. He chose a noble horse from those shown to him. Before mounting it, he remembered the Jew who was a judge of horses, and he called for him.

The Jew came, examined the horse, and said, "My king! You

must not mount this horse. He is wild, and he who rides him will be killed."

The king laughed at the Jew's words and had in mind mounting the horse. His advisors, however, suggested that one of the king's horsemen try out the horse beforehand. At first the horseman rode well; then lo! the spectators turned pale. They saw the horse begin to prance. He had become wild, and the rider, as experienced as he was, lost his balance. The wild horse threw him to the ground where he lay without a breath of life.

As a token of thanks that his life had been saved, the king gave the Jew a small coin. The Jew thanked the king and returned home.

After a short time, the Jew was called to the king again. This time the king asked him, "Tell me—who am I?"

"Who are you? You are a simple peasant, and no more," answered the Jew.

"What?" asked the king angrily, having expected praise. "How dare you talk like that to a king? I shall have you imprisoned for your insolence!" Whereupon he ordered his guards to shackle the Jew.

That night the king came to his mother, the queen, and asked her in excitement, "Mother, tell me; who am I?"

"What do you mean, who are you? You are a king and the son of a king. Your grandfather and his grandfather were kings," was the reply.

But the king was not satisfied and shouted angrily, "Tell me the truth. Who was my father?"

When his mother saw the king so excited, a great fear crept into her heart, and she revealed the truth. "You are a peasant's son."

"What are you hinting at?" asked the king in astonishment.

"Sit down, and I shall tell you. Years ago, numbering the years of your life, I gave birth to my first born son. Two days later his father, the king, died, and the next day the child died too. I grieved deeply, but before the death of my child was known, I sent one of my trusted servants to a peasant woman who had given birth to a son the very day of my own son's birth. I requested my servant to steal the peasant's child. I was a faithful mother, as you know. But you are but a peasant's son."

When the queen mother had finished speaking, the king hurried to the prison. He entered the Jew's cell and said, "I have come to set you free, but before I do so, answer me one question: Why did you say I was a peasant?"

"It is very simple," answered the Jew. "When I saved you the money you wanted to spend on the diamond necklace, you sent me off with a petty coin. I kept quiet. I saved your life, and what is more precious to a man than his own life? But you sent me off with a small coin. I kept quiet, but in my heart I knew that you were not a king. A king does not behave so. And who behaves that way? A simple peasant."

· 37 · The Right Answer to the Right Question

IFA 252. Recorded by Z. M. Haimovitsh from Elija Aharonyan, born in Persia, now a resident of the Malben Home for the Aged in Neve Haim.

On the name of Abraham's mother, see L. Ginzberg, The Legends of the Jews, *I, 186, and V, 208. Motif H561.6, "King and peasant vie in riddling questions and answers," is present and indicates that this story is a remnant of Type 921,* The King and the Peasant's Son, *a world-wide folktale.*

· ONCE IN A bitter winter, when the king was in jovial spirits after a round of drinks, he said to his minister, who was his right-hand man, "We will go and see a little of the life of our people in the cold and snow that has attacked our country."

Said the minister, "I am certain not a living soul can be found in the streets of our city now in this severe frost."

They set off, and they did not find anyone in the streets. They alighted from the coach and waited. Suddenly they felt that someone was approaching them. Asked the king, "Who are you?"

"I am a Jew," was the answer of the wanderer. His scant clothes were tattered.

"Are you not cold?" asked the king. "I am cold wearing my

warm clothes; so what about you in your meager tattered clothes?"

Answered the Jew, "The wind enters one side of my tattered clothes and goes out the other side. Whereas the wind enters your fine clothes on one side but finds no way out."

The king laughed and said to the Jew, "Come near us and warm yourself at our heater." He took out his purse and divided the money into two equal portions, saying to the Jew, "If you answer my question the proper way, you will receive half of it."

Said the Jew, "Question me, your majesty, please."

The king asked, "What was the name of the mother of Abraham the Patriarch, the Friend of God?"

"Amatlai, daughter of Karnebo," answered the Jew in a second.

"Take half of the money," ordered the king.

"Now with your kind permission, your majesty, I shall ask you a question. If you know the answer I shall give you your money back, but if not, I should like to request the rest of the money."

"Agreed," said the king.

"My mother died only four months ago, what was *her* name?"

The king laughed and said, "Take the second half of the money!"

The Jew took all the money, and the king with his minister went home happy and in a good mood.

· 38 · A Dispute in Sign Language

IFA 505. Recorded by S. Gabai from Shlomo Haim, born in Iraq.

This tale is a combination of Type 922, The Shepherd Substituting for the Priest Answers the King's Questions, episode I ("The Situation"), and Type 924A, Discussion between Priest and Jew Carried On by Symbols. For a different interpretation of the signs in a Jewish version of this tale, see M. Gaster, The Exempla of the Rabbis, No. 443, pp. 177, 269. For another version, see A. Druyanov, Vol. II, No. 2028. For a bibliography of the Arabian versions of this tale type, see V. Chauvin, Vol. VIII, p. 125, No. 112, and E. S. Stevens, No. 18, p. 89. Type 924A is dis-

cussed in R. Köhler and J. Bolte, Kleinere Schriften, *Vol. II, pp. 479–94, No. 64, "Rosenblüts Disputaziones Freiheits mit einem Juden." It has crossed to Argentina in the Spanish tradition and is currently told in the United States by American Jews.*

• ONCE THERE was a wicked priest who hated Jews. One day he summoned the chief rabbi and said to him, "I want to have a dispute with a Jew in the language of signs. I give you thirty days to prepare yourself, and if nobody appears to take part in the dispute, I shall order that all the Jews be killed."

What was the rabbi to do? He brought the bad tidings to his people and order them to fast and to pray in the synagogue. A week went by, two weeks, three weeks passed, but there was no one with the courage to accept the priest's challenge and the great responsibility. It was already the fourth week, and still there was no one to represent the Jews in the dispute.

Then along came a poultry dealer who had been away, bringing chickens from the nearby villages into the town. He had not heard what was going on there, but he noticed on his arrival that the market was closed, and at home he found his wife and children fasting, praying, and weeping.

"What is the matter?" asked the poultry dealer. His wife replied, "The wicked priest has ordered a Jew to hold a discussion with him in the language of signs. If there is no one who is able to do so, all of us will be killed."

"Is that all the matter?" wondered the poultry dealer in surprise. "Go to the rabbi, and tell him that I am ready to participate."

"What are you talking about? How can you understand the priest? Greater and wiser men than you have not been willing to take upon themselves this task!" cried his wife.

"Why should you worry? In any case we shall all be killed." And off they went together to the rabbi.

"Rabbi," said the man, "I am ready to meet the priest!"

The rabbi blessed him. "May God help you and bring you success."

So the priest was told that a Jew, sent by the rabbi, would hold a discussion with him in sign language.

"You have to understand my signs and to answer them in the same way," explained the priest to the Jew before a great assembly. Then he pointed a finger to him. In reply the Jew pointed two fingers. Then the priest took a piece of white cheese from his pocket. In reply the Jew took out an egg. Then the priest took the seeds of some grain and scattered them on the floor. In reply, the Jew set a hen free from the coop and let it eat up the seeds.

"Well done," exclaimed the priest in amazement. "You answered my questions correctly." And he gave the poultry dealer many gifts and ordered his servant to bathe him and to give him fine garments to wear.

"Now I know that the Jews are wise men, if the most humble among them was able to understand me," admitted the priest.

The town was in great excitement, and the people waited in suspense for the result of the dispute. When they saw the poultry dealer leaving the priest's house in fine garments and with a happy expression on his face, they understood that everything was in order, blessed be the Almighty.

"How did it go? What did the priest ask you?" all the people wanted to know. The rabbi called the poultry dealer to his home and asked him to relate what had happened.

And this is what the poultry dealer related: "The priest pointed with one finger to my eyes, meaning to take out my eye. I pointed with two fingers to imply, I would take out both his eyes. Then he took out a piece of cheese to show that I was hungry while he had cheese. So I took out an egg to show that I was not in need of his alms. Then he spilled some wheat grain on the floor. So I fed my hen, knowing it was hungry and thinking what a pity to waste the grain."

At the same time the priest's friends questioned him. "What did you ask the Jew? What did he reply?"

The priest related: "At first I pointed one finger, meaning that there is only one king. He pointed with two fingers, meaning that there are two kings, the king in heaven and the king on earth. Then I took out a piece of cheese, meaning, Is this cheese from a white or a black goat? In answer he took out an egg, meaning, Is this egg from a white or a brown hen? Finally I scattered some grain on the floor, meaning that the Jews are spread all over the world. Whereupon he freed his hen which ate up all the grain, meaning that the Messiah will come and gather all the Jews from the four corners of the world."

· 39 ·   Charity Will Save from Death

IFA 250. Recorded by Mila Ohel, a Hebrew University student, from Menachem Kamus, born in Libya.

The funeral custom described in this tale is practised in Israel at the present time. For the origin of the phrase that is called out, see Prov. 10:2 and 11:4. Type 1699, Misunderstanding because of Ignorance of Foreign Language, similarly involves persons of differing cultures and languages. Motif A661.0.1.2, "Saint Peter as porter of heaven," is here applied to a Moslem porter. For a Palestinian tale in which St. Peter acts as porter of heaven, see H. Schmidt-P. Kahle, II, 137. Other motifs present in this tale are A661.0.1, "Gate of heaven," K2371.1, "Heaven entered by a trick," K890, "Dupe tricked into killing himself," and J2496.2, "Misunderstanding because of lack of knowledge of a different language other than one's own."

· Whenever a Jewish funeral used to take place, a certain Moslem always heard the words *Tsedaka tatsil mimaveth* (Charity will save from death! Charity will save from death) being called out. However, he could not make out the word *tsedaka* (charity), and he thought they said *taka,* which means "portal" in Arabic.

The Moslem could not understand why the Jews were calling out about a portal during a funeral. He had a friend who was a Jew. He went to him and said, "I want to ask you something. If you tell me, I will do you many good turns; if not, I will despise you from this day onward."

"Go ahead," said the Jew.

The Moslem asked, "Why is it that amongst you they say during a burial, *Taka, Taka?*"

The Jew understood what the Moslem was referring to and

answered, "Sir, that is a very great religious secret, and I am not able to reveal it. If I do, my Jewish brethren will kill me."

The Moslem said to him, "My brother, I swear in the name of Allah and his prophet that not a single man, neither Jew nor Moslem, will know that you have revealed the secret."

The Moslem pleaded and pleaded, and the Jew was not able to get rid of him; so he said, "Good. I will disclose it, sir. As you probably know, the Garden of Eden is reserved for Moslems only, and there is no entrance there for Jews or for Christians, as the key is in Moslem hands. What can we do? We Jews also want to enter the Garden of Eden. Now there is a secret known only to us! Above the gateway there is a small portal through which a soul can push its way and thus enter the Garden. Hence when a Jew dies, the people following his coffin call out to remind him about the *taka,* the portal above the gate, which is locked and bolted so that no one can push it aside and come in."

When the Moslem was told about "*Taka,*" the portal, he was cheerful, but mingled with his joy was anger against the Jews, so cunningly deceiving the watchman of the Moslem Paradise.

Day by day he became more and more angry, until he decided he would have his revenge on the cursed Jews and close up the portal, their single entry to the Garden of Eden.

He said in his heart, "If I kill myself, I will go to the Garden of Eden, and knowing the secret, I will take stones, sand, and water and block up the portal over the gate so the Jews will no longer be able to enter." Whereupon he took a dagger and stabbed himself to death.

They arranged a big funeral and buried him. And until today he is still busy filling up the portal over the gate of Paradise. Who knows when he will finish his task?

· 40 ·   *Settling an Account with a Joker*

IFA 332. Recorded by Yehuda Karyu from Shlomo Benvenisti, born in Turkey.

The biblical verse referred to by the Armenian is Gen. 49:14.

According to the Midrash, the tribe of Zebulun used ships for commerce and so supported the tribe of Issachar, which devoted itself to the study of the Torah. See L. Ginzberg, The Legends of the Jews, *VII, 245, 512.*

• IN THE CITY of Istanbul, an Armenian pedlar used to hawk glassware. It was his custom to tie up his loaded ass outside the shop of Zebulun the Jew. One and the same joke was always on the pedlar's lips the moment his eyes fell on Zebulun. "Your brother is asking to talk to you." And he would point his finger to the ass laden with glassware.

It was painful for Zebulun to hear this, as his little brother, Issachar, was a wise man and a scholar. The Armenian used to accompany his joke with a few words of "consolation." "What is the matter? Why are you in a temper? Is it not written in your Holy Scriptures: "Issachar, a bony ass!"

The Turkish neighbor of Zebulun would always ask him, "Why, once and for all, do you not make a retort to the Armenian?"

"Time will have something to say," was Zebulun's usual answer, and within his heart he was preparing a plan of vengeance.

One morning Zebulun rose early with his pockets crammed with horseflies. He peered along the road, looking out for the pedlar. And along came the pedlar strolling behind his ass, now even more heavily laden than usual. The pedlar's tongue already turned over the familiar joke. "Zebulun, Zebulun, your brother is asking to talk to you." And his finger pointed to the ass.

"Yes, yes," answered Zebulun. "I have in mind whispering something into my brother's ear."

The pedlar felt that a double pleasure was awaiting him this time, and he exclaimed, "Talk, talk, Zebulun. Your brother is listening to you!"

Zebulun approached the animal, leaned over his ear, and filled it with horseflies. It did not take long. The ass jumped and leaped like a champion. The glassware slid down from his back, falling on the ground with a tinkling crash and a shower of fragments, big and small.

The Armenian pedlar brought a law case against Zebulun,

charging him with responsibility for the loss of all his goods and money.

Zebulun turned to the judge and said, "Your worship, from early morning this man stands before my shop and points to his ass, saying he is my brother. Your worship, we have a little sister in full bloom. Her wedding is drawing near. When I whispered the wedding date to my brother and reminded him not to be late, the poor animal was so delighted that he started to dance for joy."

Turning to the Armenian with a smile, the Turkish judge declared: "The Jew is discharged. You cannot blame a man for inviting his brother to his sister's wedding. Now you know what may happen to anyone who makes a mockery of his fellowman."

• *41* •   *The Cunning of the Sons of Israel*

IFA 249. Recorded by Mila Ohel in 1952 from Menachem Kamus, born in Libya.

This tale suggests stories in the United States of Yankee tricks (cf. R. M. Dorson, Jonathan Draws the Long Bow [*Cambridge, Mass., 1946*], *pp. 78–94*). *It belongs under the general Motif K500, "Escape from death or danger by deception."*

• THIS IS A tale of a pedlar who managed to sell all his goods in the village, and on the third day of the week he was on his way home, happy and lighthearted.

Suddenly an armed robber appeared in front of him and said, "Give me all you have, and save your soul."

"By my life!" said the Jew laughing, "I have nothing with me, my master, just a donkey. Take it!"

Said the robber: "Unbeliever, I do not need a donkey. Give me a cigarette, and go on in peace."

Said the Jew, "By my life, my master, I do not smoke. If I did I would give you all the cigarettes I had."

Said the robber: "Villain! I do not want anything from you; just tell me one thing, you damned one. What is the meaning of 'The Cunning of the Sons of Israel'?" The Jew was afraid. What could he tell the robber? How could he explain to him this verse from the Torah?

"My master," he said, "ask me whatever you like but not this. It is a holy thing among us, from our Torah, and I do not even know how to explain it."

Said the robber, "Either you explain it and go on your way in peace, or you will find your grave here, like a dog!"

The Jew saw that the robber would kill him if he did not tell him something. He thought and thought and then found a way. "My master, I will tell you this thing, but promise and swear that you will not reveal it to anyone!"

The Jew took out a reel of thread from his coat, pulled out the end of the thread, and handed it to the robber with these words: "My master, in order to know what the secret is, you must hold the thread and wait here until you feel a sharp pull. Then go with the thread until you reach a certain place, and there you will find out the secret."

The robber held the end of the thread and stood ready. The Jew mounted his donkey and set off quickly, unwinding the thread as he went. When he had finished one reel he took out a second one and joined the ends of both the reels. When he had finished unwinding the second reel, he took out a third one and bound the end of the thread to a tree. Then he hurried to the town, and soon he arrived home.

In this way the robber learned the meaning of 'The Cunning of the Sons of Israel.' And of course, he kept his promise and told nobody about it.

•42• *A Tale of a Jew Who Bridled the Wind*

IFA. 142. Recorded by Zvi Moshe Haimovitch, director of the Malben Home for the Aged in Neve Haim, from Elija David, a resident of that home, who was born in Basra, Iraq.

For another version of this tale, in which the city smoke is bridled, see A. Druyanov, Vol. II, No. 1995. The general Motifs H500, "Test of cleverness or ability," H960, "Tasks performed through cleverness," and H1020, "Tasks contrary to the laws of nature," are popular in Jewish test tales.

• THERE WAS once a king who had three viziers: a Jew, a Moslem, and a Christian. The king venerated his Jewish vizier above all of them because of his great wisdom; he could always find a way out of any difficulty.

The other two viziers, the Christian and the Moslem, always sought ways to belittle the Jew in the king's eyes. The king, however, was clever and did not pay attention to their intrigues. He used to say, "The Jew is wiser than you!"

"Are we stupid in your eyes?" they asked.

"No, you are not stupid, but a Jew is wiser. The righteousness of these words will be proved by a Jew himself."

One day the king ordered his servants, "Stand at the market place and charge the first Moslem passing by, 'You have stolen from the king the wind and the air encircling the earth.'"

The king's servants did as they were bidden. They stood at the market place until they saw a Moslem. Instantly they caught hold of him, charged him, and brought him before the king. The king blamed the Moslem, accusing him of having stolen the wind and the air. The Moslem pleaded with the king for mercy, swearing that he was not guilty of this offense.

Said the king, "If you want to be forgiven, do as I bid you. I shall hand you the wind. Do as you like with it, and in four months time, let me know what you have done."

Four months passed, and the Moslem appeared before the king. He had but one request. "Forgive me my king! I did not know what to do with the wind. Indeed," he pleaded, "I am blowing on my hands, and not a sign of the wind remains."

The king sent the Moslem away and ordered his servant to catch hold of the first Christian at the market place and to charge him with the same offense. The servants did as they were bidden. They went to the market place and waited until they saw a Christian. Instantly they caught hold of him, charged him, and brought him before the king. The king accused the Christian of having stolen the wind and the air. The Christian fell at the king's feet and begged for mercy. The king sent him off, urging him to make use of the wind and to report back in four months time.

Four months passed by, and the trembling Christian came to the king's palace with tears in his eyes. He begged for mercy, saying he did not know what to do with the wind. The king forgave him and sent him away. Then he said to his servants, "Go to the market, catch hold of the first Jew you set your eyes on, and charge him with the same offense."

The king's servants did as they were bidden. They stood at the market place and waited until they saw a Jew. A poor and shabby man he was, indeed. Instantly they caught hold of him. He did not seem worried at all on hearing the offense he was being charged with, and when he appeared before the king, he said, "Of course I can bridle the wind and make use of it, but I need three things. I need a written authorization. I need a sum of money for preparation and clothing, for of what esteem will I be in the eyes of the world if I am shabby? Lastly, I need a team of workers and clerks to carry out the project."

The king immediately ordered clerks to prepare the certificate and agreed to fulfill all the Jew's conditions.

In no time the Jew opened a big office with clerks and workers. Then he ordered all the houseowners and shopkeepers to come to his office. When they appeared, he ordered them to shut all the windows of their flats and shops.

"How will we be able to breathe?" they asked him in amazement.

The Jew answered, "The wind and the air are mine, by order of the king. Here is his signed certificate. If you want to breathe, you must pay a tax." So the Jew collected a large sum of money. He also prohibited jewelers from using bellows and owners of sailing vessels from using the wind, without paying a tax.

The Jew put the money he collected into safes together with copies of receipts he had given against payments. Clerks kept the accounts and handed over reports of all the expenses and of the Jew's profits from exploiting the wind.

Four months passed by, and the Jew went to the palace with his profits. The king, arrayed in fine clothes, called his viziers, the judges, as well as the Moslem and the Christian who did not fulfil their missions.

The king asked the Christian, "Why did you not carry out my orders?"

The Christian answered, "I could not control the wind." The Moslem gave a similar reply.

The king called the Jew and asked him, "What did you do with the wind I gave you?"

The Jew gave details of what he had done in the four months at his disposal and the large sum of money that enlarged the king's treasury from the use of the wind.

The king was delighted with the Jew's cleverness and said to his viziers, the judges, "You see, the cleverness of a Jew is greater than yours; that is why I revere a Jew!"

The king appointed his Jewish vizier as his chief advisor and the poor Jew as his financial advisor. From that day no one dared to talk against Jews in the whole kingdom.

·43·   The Kingdom of the Lazy People

IFA 423. Recorded by Azaria Alkalai, a high-school student, from his mother, who was born in Bulgaria.

The name Oved has no meaning to Bulgarians hearing it in Spanish, the language in which the tale was narrated. But it is a common name in the Bible, and in Hebrew it retains the meaning of laborer. In Jewish tradition Noah is the culture-hero who teaches people how to till the land. For references to these legends, see L. Ginzberg, The Legends of the Jews, *I, 167, V, 190. Motifs A541, "Cultural hero teaches arts and crafts," A1441.4, "Origin of sowing and planting," and W111, "Laziness," provide contrasting themes. Dov Noy discusses "Jewish Folktales on Agriculture" (Hebrew), in* Machnayim, *No. 53 (1961).*

• IN A CERTAIN far-off land there was a kingdom of idlers. All day long the people dug the ground for gold, hoping to become rich. For years and years they went on digging, but they did not find anything. They were sad, and their king became angry and bad-tempered. But they still disdained honest work.

One day a young man happened to pass by. He was cheerful and good-humored. He walked in a carefree way, and on his lips was a merry song. When the diggers saw him, they asked him to stop whistling: "Our king is very angry and bad-tempered. He may even kill you," they warned him. The young man laughed, "Be it so; just bring me to him."

The diggers stopped their work and took the young man to the king's palace. On the way they asked him, "What is your name?"

"Oved (worker)," answered the young man.

"And why do you whistle?"

"Because I am cheerful and content."

"And why are you cheerful and content?"

"Because I have a lot of gold."

Hearing this they were filled with joy and told the king about the gold. The king asked Oved, "Is it true that you have a hoard of gold?"

"Yes!" was the answer. "I have seven sacks full of gold."

The king became very excited, and he immediately called his people and ordered them to bring the sacks. But Oved explained, "It will take time to get the gold, my king. It is kept in a cave, guarded by a seven-headed ogre. Only I myself can take it out from there. Give me all your people for one year, and during that time we will free the gold from the monster."

The king had no alternative. He put horses, oxen, and men at Oved's disposal and commanded the people to carry out the young man's instructions.

Oved ordered his men to bring plows and to plow the rich and fertile land of the country. Then, after plowing, they sowed, and at harvest season they collected seven wagons full of the finest wheat.

All the while the king warned Oved that if he did not bring him the sacks of gold at the end of the year, he would be beheaded. Whereon Oved smiled and explained, "We need wheat to block up the mouth of the monster," and he continued to be cheerful and to sing merry songs.

For seven days Oved wandered with his seven wagons until he

reached a large town whose land had no vegetation. When the merchants of the town saw the wagons of ripe wheat, they paid a large sum of money in exchange—seven sacks full of gold. After seven more days had passed, Oved once again came before the king, who asked him, "Have you succeeded in overcoming the monster?"

Oved answered with a smile, "I sold the wheat to people whose soil is barren, and in return I was given seven sacks of gold."

When the king heard Oved's story, he said to him in excitement, "He who tills the earth provides the bread. Indeed, we can get out of our good earth even more than seven sacks of gold each year." And he asked Oved to stay in his kingdom and rule his citizens.

Oved, however, refused, saying "There are many men in this world who do not know the secret of labor. One can dig gold from the earth by tilling it, sowing golden wheat, and turning it into bread. It is my duty to reveal this secret to others too."

Cheerfully and happily Oved set off on his wanderings.

·44·   *The Great Lie*

IFA 342. Recorded by Naim Daniel, a laborer, from Ezra Tsalah, born in Iraq.

A text related to Types 1920C, The Master and the Peasant: the Great Ox, 1920F, He Who Says "That's a Lie" Must Pay a Fine, and 852, The Hero Forces the Princess To Say "That is a Lie." Cf. Motifs X905.1, "Master brought to say 'You lie,'" and H509.5, "Test: telling skillful lie." Type 1920, Contest in Lying, is represented in No. 24 (in this book), "The Tall Tale of the Merchant's Son" (IFA 7). In the present tale the liars' contest is given a serious historical setting.

A Turkish version is given in W. Eberhard–P. N. Boratav, No. 363, and Sephardic Jewish examples can be found in A. D. L. Palacin, Nos. 19 and 124. This tale type, which appears in the Book of Achikar, is discussed by Jan de Vries, in "Die Märchen von Klügen Rätsellosern, eine vergleichende Untersuchung"

(*Folklore Fellows Communications*, No. 73 [*Helsinki*, *1928*]),
pp. 375–76.

• MANY, MANY YEARS AGO there lived a king who very much loved
the Jews of his country. In times of trouble the king used to turn
to the rabbi for advice and help, and the rabbi used to resolve the
problems willingly and to the king's satisfaction.

The ministers envied the rabbi and decided to blacken his name
so that the king would no longer honor him. Day after day they
related to the king evil stories about the rabbi; the king, however,
refused to believe them. They continued to persuade the king,
"You must rid our state of the Jews. They despise the king and
disobey his orders."

One day the king informed his ministers, "Anyone who comes
to me and spins a tale that is entirely fictitious and contains not a
word of truth, will receive from my treasury a prize of one thousand pounds."

The ministers made the king's challenge known amongst the
people, and every one, including the ministers, decided to make
up a tall story. The king heard all the tales, but in each one there
was a grain of truth. The storytellers, and the ministers among
them, hung their heads in shame. Not one of them succeeded in
winning the prize.

Time passed, and one day a humble Jew came to the rabbi's
room and told him he wanted to compete for the king's prize.
The rabbi advised him to go to the king. First, however, the Jew
went to the market and bought a large clay jar. Only then did
he go to the palace. The king was informed that a humble Jew
had come and wanted to tell him a story. The king gave orders
to let him enter; whereupon the Jew came in and told this story:

"My king! Your father and my father, blessed be their memory,
were partners in pickling cucumber. One day your father proclaimed a war against a country that despised his rule. During
the war that followed your father requested my father to lend
him a clay jar filled with golden pounds. My father, who was his
friend and also his partner, fulfilled his request and lent him a
large jar full of money." The Jew showed the jar to the king and
continued: "My father left this jar in a hole with a note inside it

giving us advice if we should ever come down in the world: 'Go to the king, or his heir, and request that he pay the debt due to us from old times until day.' My king! At present our position is very bad, and we have not even the money to buy bread. For this reason I was obliged to come to you and request that you pay the debt."

When the king heard this story from the lips of the Jew, he was very confused, and did not know how to answer him. If the story were true, he would have to fill up the jar with golden coins, which meant more than five thousand pounds. But if it was just a tall tale and a great lie, he would have to had over only one thousand pounds.

The king requested fifteen minutes so as to consult his ministers. Of course they advised him to tell the Jew that his story was a lie and to pay him the thousand pounds. The king told the Jew that there was not a single word of truth in his story. So the humble Jew won the prize, which was duly paid to him at the treasury.

When the Jew left, the king was angry with his ministers and told them never to complain about the Jews again, because they were the shrewdest of all people. And from that time on, it was forbidden to say a single bad word against the rabbi.

On the way from the palace the humble Jew called on the rabbi and told him the story. The rabbi was overjoyed and gave him another thousand pounds as a present. So a humble Jew saved his brethren from the hands of evildoers.

·45· *The Bakalawa Story*

IFA 13. Recorded by Elisheva Schoenfeld in Affula in 1956 from Isaac Al-Bahri, born in Turkey.

Type 1626, Dream Bread. Motif K444, "Dream bread: the most wonderful dream," is very popular in Mediterranean folk-litera-ture, and the cunning winner always belongs to the same people (race, religion) as the storyteller and his listeners. Other IFA versions of this tale type originate in Afghanistan, Turkey, Mo-

rocco, and Iraq. This tale is reported throughout Europe, from India, Japan, and the French, English, Spanish, and Portuguese traditions in America. Central Asian texts are printed in M. I. Shewerdin, Vol. II, No. 141, and W. Sidelnikov, Nos. 18, 40. A Caucasian example is given in A. H. Bjazirov, No. 42.

• A CHRISTIAN, a Jew, and a Moslem went to Istanbul to try their luck. Time passed, and they wanted to sleep. It was very cold, and each of them was keen to sleep in the middle, as it was warmer there between the others.

The Jew said, "It is written in the Holy Torah that I must sleep in the middle."

The Christian and Moslem wondered.

"Look," continued the Jew. "You, Suleiman, celebrate your Sabbath on Friday. You, George, celebrate yours on Sunday, but mine is in the middle, on Saturday. As my feast day is in the middle, my place to sleep must also be in the middle."

The other two agreed to this, and the Jew snuggled up to sleep between the two of them.

When they reached Istanbul, they found a golden coin in the street and started to discuss what to do with it. The Jew kept quiet. The Christian and Moslem decided after a long quarrel and much talking that with the money they could buy a *bakalawa,* a sweet Turkish cake, and the one who dreamed the most beautiful dream would eat it in the morning.

In the night the Jew woke up and felt very hungry. He tasted the cake. He tried to awaken his friends, but they were sound asleep and did not hear him. The Jew went to sleep for an hour; then again he woke up and ate another piece of the cake. He tried again to awaken his friends, but again he was unsuccessful. So he continued to nibble at the cake all night until not a morsel remained.

In the morning the three friends went to a cafe in the market. Many people were assembled there: Moslems, Christians, and Jews. Suleiman told them what had happened—how they had found a golden coin in the street and spent it on a *bakalawa.* Now they wanted the people to judge who had dreamt the most beautiful dream.

The Christian told his dream first. "I dreamt that Jesus himself came to me and carried me on his wings to the Garden of Eden. When we arrived there, he pointed out to me all the saints sitting around and entertaining each other."

Then it was Suleiman's turn. "I dreamt that Mohammed himself appeared before me and took me to have a look at the Garden of Eden. Is there any dream more beautiful than that?" he asked the people.

When the Jew's turn came, he said, "My dream was different from yours. Unfortunately, I was not lucky enough to visit the Garden of Eden as both of you did. But Moses, our lawgiver came to me and said, 'Suleiman is with his master, Mohammed in Mecca, George is with his master, Jesus in Nazareth. Who knows if either of them will return or not?' And he advised me to eat the *bakalawa.*"

"Did you eat it?" they asked eagerly.

"Of course," came the answer. "Do you think that I disobey our lawgiver's advice!"

Part VI
Husbands and Wives

·46· *Years Are as Days*

IFA 144. Recorded by Zvi Moshe Haimovitch from Serl Roch-feld, born in Poland.

Type 1588**, Cheater Caught by Seizing on His Own Words. The general Motifs J21, "Counsels proved wise by experience," and J154, "Wise words of dying father," are both present in this tale and specify a series of warnings. These do not, however, include the warning "Do not mix with redheaded people." Beliefs about bad luck associated with redheaded women are given in Popular Beliefs and Superstitions from North Carolina, *ed. W. D. Hand ("Frank C. Brown Collection of North Carolina Folklore," Vol. 6 [Durham, N.C., 1961]), Nos. 3795, 3796.*

Motif J21 is central to Type 910, Precepts Bought or Given Prove Correct. Cf. Jewish literary versions given in M. Gaster, Exempla of the Rabbis, *Nos. 367, 402; Gaster (ed.),* Ma'aseh Book, *No. 198; M. J. Bin Gorion, Der Born Judas, III, 100. Cf. M. I. Shewerdin, Vol. II. Nos. 100, 105 (from central Asia); and A. D. L. Palacin, No. 121 (Sephardic-Jewish).*

• WHEN THE HOUR came for Rabbi Zishe to depart from this world, he called his son and said to him, "Listen, my son; my hour has come. I have but one request to make before returning to the Almighty God his deposit—my soul. I want to warn you not to mix with evil people. Keep away from them, especially from redheads, the offspring of Laban Haarami, as they would surely try to deceive you. If, God forbid, this should happen, look at once for another readhead and ask his advice, because only he can save you from trouble."

After saying this, Rabbi Zishe returned his soul to God. As his wife had been dead for many years, his son was an orphan. After a short time good people came to visit him and wanted to make a match between him and the daughter of the rich Reb Fishel. The young girl had a good name in town and was said to be honest, beautiful, and perfect in every way. But alas! She was redheaded like her father.

The orphan, a Yeshiva student, obliged to dine at the tables of the well-to-do, refused to marry the girl on account of his father's warning. However, what brains cannot do, time will do. His position became worse from day to day, and as he had no alternative, he gave in at last and agreed to the marriage. He made just one condition, that Reb Fishel should give him board for ten years besides the dowry. Reb Fishel did not hesitate and promised even more.

Ten days had not passed after the marriage when the wealthy Reb Fishel informed his son-in-law that he would no longer give him board.

"What I have promised I have fulfilled," he said. "As the meaning of the word 'days' in the Torah is also 'years,' the number of years which I promised you has already passed."

Once again the son-in-law found himself in great trouble, and no one knew how to advise him. Then he remembered the words of his father, whereupon he went out on the roadside, and stopping the first redhead on the way, he emptied all the bitterness of his heart to him.

The *gingy* listened quietly and said without anger, "Go immediately to the deceiver, your father-in-law, and tell him you have decided to divorce his daughter. When he asks why, tell him that according to Jewish law it is permitted to divorce a woman who does not give birth within ten years, and according to him, days are as years."

Reb Fishel turned pale when he heard the decision of his son-in-law. He began pleading with him not to bring such shame upon him and promised to set aside his decision. At last the son-in-law agreed to go on with the marriage but on condition that a considerable sum of money should be put in his name in the bank, as well as a guarantee to insure the promises of his father-in-law.

From that time on the young couple lived a life of peace and comfort.

The Clever Wife

IFA 506. Recorded by S. Gabai from Simah Hagoli, born in Iraq.
Motif L162, "Lowly heroine marries prince (king)," usually
requires a demonstration of cleverness by the heroine prior to the
marriage itself. This motif appears in Types 870–79, The Heroine
Marries the Prince. *However, in the present tale, the clever act*
comes after the marriage. Motifs F1041.1.4, "Death from longing,"
and D1624, "Image bleeding," are present. For Turkish versions,
see W. Eberhard-P. N. Boratav, No. 305, "Die Wachspuppe."

• ONCE THERE was a king who was ready to marry, on condition
that his wife would break off relations with her parents after
marriage and never see them again. Many beautiful girls were
eager to marry the king, and time and again he chose from
amongst them the one most befitting him.

One, two, and three weeks would pass, while the king was very
busy attending receptions and audiences. His wife was always
left alone at home, and she had no one to speak to. After several
months of suffering the wife would pass away. The king used to
mourn his wife's death, and then, after a short time, he would
proclaim a new contest for a bride.

This went on for a long time. Queen succeeded queen, and not
one of them was able to bear up for more than a few months. At
last there came a lovely, clever girl who wished to marry the king.
Her parents were against the match, especially her mother.

"My beloved only daughter. It is difficult for me to throw you
into the fire," she said. "The king is a woman-killer, because of
his harsh treatment. At first he buries his wife in the castle and
then in a grave. If you marry him, you will bury me together
with yourself."

"Do not be afraid, mother," the daughter consoled her. "The
king will bury neither you nor me. I will settle everything, if
you have patience."

At last the mother gave in. Her daughter was the only one to find favor in the king's eyes, and she won the contest. In due course she married him and was parted from her parents. After two days, however, she became bored, as the king was always preoccupied with his duties. Indeed, it was difficult for her to become accustomed to the silent house without a soul to talk to.

What did she do? She took the skin of a goat, blew it up, dressed it in clothes, drew a face, and put a hat on its head. It looked like a man indeed. Afterward she placed the stuffed doll on a chair and began relating to it all that weighed on her heart and troubled her.

One month passed, two months went by, and the woman did not change her habit. When her husband came home, she used to talk to him cheerfully, and while he was away, she used to play with her doll.

The king did not know how his wife managed to bear up for so long. Three months passed, four months went by, and the king decided to look into the matter. What did he do? He bored a small hole in the wall of her room, and lo, what did he see? His wife sitting with a stranger, talking to him. "Unfaithful one!" he said in his heart. "She has been deceiving me all the time."

He decided to take his revenge and afflict her and her lover with severe and terrible sufferings. He behaved as if he knew nothing of the matter, but he gave orders to the watchman to be on the lookout for anyone trying to leave the palace. In the evening the watchman reported that not a single person had left the palace. Then after dinner, the king suggested to his wife, "Come, let us look around the house and inspect your rooms." At last they reached the chamber where the king had watched his wife conversing with a man. Suddenly the king stopped and drew out a dagger. "Where have you hidden your lover?" he asked.

The queen showed him the doll hidden in the cupboard. The king stabbed it with his dagger, whereupon blood poured out.

"What is this?" the king asked. "If it is a doll, where does the blood come from?"

"That is my sorrow and grief, O king. I told my doll all that there was in my heart. Otherwise I myself would have burst from suffering."

At last the king understood that he himself had caused the

death of his former wives and that his present wife was the cleverest of them all. He decided to revoke his decree and allowed his wife to visit her parents. You can imagine the rejoicing of the mother and her daughter.

• 48 • The Deceived Girl and the Stone of Suffering

IFA 155. Recorded by Sara Bashari, Yemenite-born high-school student, in Kefar Saba in 1957 from Leah Nakhshon, born near Sadda, southeastern Yemen.

Type 894, The Ghoulish Schoolmaster and the Stone of Pity. W. Eberhard and P. N. Boratav list thirty-eight Turkish variants, No. 185, "Der Geduldstein II." This tale is very popular in Oriental folk literature. The transformation of the stone of patience into a beast, as in the present text, is unusual. In most versions the stone bursts as it loses its patience. Cf. Motif K1911, "The false bride (substitute bride)." Other Motifs present are K2251.1, "Treacherous slave-girl," and H13.2.2, "Recognition by overheard conversation with stone." Type 894 is reported from India, Persia, Egypt, and eastern and southern Europe. An Uzbekistan variant is given in M. I. Shewerdin, Vol. II, No. 74.

• A RICH AND respected family had an only daughter whom they looked upon as the apple of their eye. One night the girl dreamed a fearful dream. An old man with a long white beard falling to his knees appeared before her. He proclaimed: "For seven years you will be hungry, and however much you eat, you will still be hungry. Seven years of thirst will follow, and no matter what you drink, you will remain thirsty. Then you will spend seven years more tending a dead man in a locked-up house. Only after twenty-one years of suffering will happiness come your way and be with you until the end of your days."

The frightened girl recounted her dream to her parents, who became terrified. After a few days she began to feel famished.

Her parents spent all their money on food and kept selling their property until they were impoverished. Still they could not satisfy their daughter's hunger. The fond mother wandered with her daughter from town to town and from village to village, asking for food.

Seven long years of hunger, misery, and exhaustion passed, and the mother continued to wander with her daughter. Now began the years of thirst. The daughter was always thirsty. Her thirst became greater and greater and could not be quenched, not even by rivers and streams. So the two of them wandered from town to village and from village to town, from mountain to valley and from valley to mountain. Everywhere the daughter drank water, yet her thirst was not quenched.

Seven years of thirst, hardship, and suffering passed, and one day the mother and daughter reached an isolated place in the desert. They saw there a house of several stories that looked like a king's palace. The house was open, and the girl asked her mother to wait while she went inside. As she entered the house, the doors were bolted behind her, and she found herself in a room where a dead man was lying on a bed.

She realized that she had ended the seven years of thirst and come to the years of exhausting care of the dead man. She knelt down and bathed and embalmed him. Then she washed and cleaned his clothes and aired the room. Day after day she carried on the burden of this work. And all the time the corpselike body did not stir from its place.

The mother, knowing of her daughter's fate, came to live in the nearest town so as to follow her doings.

The years of suffering had nearly come to an end. The girl was exhausted from the hard work and on the point of a breakdown. Then one day she saw a pretty young girl on the road in front of the house. She called out to her, threw a rope down below, and pulled her inside the house. From that time the young girl started to help her with the work.

One day, when the daughter was in the adjacent room, she heard voices. The young girl was speaking to the sick man, who had recovered from his deathlike sleep. The man asked, "Was it you who cared for me all this long time?"

"Yes!" came the positive answer.

The man continued: "You have suffered enough for me. From now on your burden will be lifted from you. You will be the queen of this house—my beloved companion."

"For days and nights I did not close my eyes," said the girl. "How good that the long and exhausting torture will come to an end!"

"Did you bear all this anguish alone?" asked the man.

"Indeed, I had a helper," answered the young girl's voice, "but she was wicked."

The daughter understood that after bearing her miserable fate for twenty-one years, she had been cheated by the pretty young girl.

The wedding day of the man drew near. All the time the poor daughter worked hard, at the orders of the young girl. One day the man decided to go to the nearby town to make purchases for the household and for the wedding. So he asked the daughter, too, who had suffered so much, what she would like him to bring her. He also informed her that she would no longer have to work after his marriage.

The daughter asked, "Bring me, my master, the stone of suffering."

The master had never heard about this precious stone, but he promised to bring it, and after much searching, he at last succeeded in procuring it. He was told by the merchant that he who reveals all sufferings of his past to this stone brings it to life; whereupon it swallows up the storyteller.

The man was very surprised that the girl had asked for this stone. After he had given it to her, he hid behind the door and heard her entire story, which began, "Alas! stone of suffering. Years of hunger passed over me, then years of thirst grieved me, then years of care. . . ."

The story was a long one, and all the time the stone became bigger and bigger. Suddenly the door opened, and the man caught the stone before it turned to life. In a trembling voice the man asked, "Why did you not tell me that she was only the servant who helped you for a few days and you were the one who suffered? How good that the truth has been revealed to me at last.

To you and only to you will belong all the joys of happiness and delight."

At the magnificent wedding that took place, the mother and many guests were present. And the wicked young girl? She disappeared, and the couple did not see her any more, all the days of their happy life.

• 49 • *With God's Will All Is Possible*

IFA 335. Recorded by Simha Gabai, an elementary-school teacher, from her father, born in Baghdad, Iraq.

Type 930, The Prophecy, episodes I–III. Of the versions of this tale type in IFA, some contain only Motif K511, "Uriah letter changed, falsified order of execution," and some only Motif K1612, "Message of death fatal to sender" (Gang nach dem Eisenhammer). See Dov Noy, "The First Thousand Folktales in the Israeli Folktales Archives," Fabula, IV (1961), 107. Arabic literary versions of this tale type are cited in V. Chauvin, VIII, 145–47, and Turkish examples can be found in W. Eberhard-P. N. Boratav, No. 125, "Der Uriasbrief." African texts are reported in C. Velten, Märchen und Erzählung der Suahili (Berlin, 1898), p. 198.

The European versions of this tale are usually combined with Type 461, Three Hairs from the Devil's Beard, as in Grimm's tale No. 29, "The Devil with Three Golden Hairs." A. Aarne wrote a monograph on this tale type, "Der reiche Mann und sein Schwiegersohn" (Folklore Fellows Communications, No. 23 [1915]), pp. 1–109. See also K. Krohn, "Übersicht uber einige Resultate der Märchenforschung" (Folklore Fellows Communications, No. 96 [1931]), pp. 57–62. S. Thompson in The Folktale, p. 139, summarizes the literary history of this tale from the study of V. Tille, "Das Märchen vom Schicksal Kind," Zeitschrift des Vereins für Volkskunde, XXIX (1919), 22–40. Tille sees India as the tale's oldest literary home. Type 930 has reached North America in French, Spanish, and Negro traditions.

See also W. Sidelnikov, No. 51 (from Kazakhstan); H. S. Bgazhda, Son of the Deer . . . , No. 21 (from Abkhazia);

*A. D. L. Palacin, No. 111 (Sephardic-Jewish); M. J. Bin Gorion,
Der Born Judas, I, 219 (Jewish literary version).*

• ONE DAY THE king and his minister went for a tour, disguised as
civilians. They wandered in the fields, and suddenly they saw far
off on a high hillock an old long-bearded man wearing a cloak.
The man wrote notes and then threw them away. The king knew
at once that the man was a holy dervish. "Come, let us see what
he is doing," he suggested to his minister.

The two of them approached the dervish, and the king asked,
"What are all these notes that you are writing? Why are you
throwing them away?"

"My king," answered the dervish. "I sit here, write notes, and
throw them away. In the first note I asked who you and your
comrade were, and straight away I knew that you were the king
and this was your minister. From the second note I learned that a
daughter was born to you last week and at the same time a son
was born to a poor woman living in the nearby town. Your
daughter is destined for this boy, and he will be your son-in-law,
my king.

"A bridegroom has been born for my daughter?" mocked the
king, and he begged for the address of this family so as to know
if the dervish's words were right. The king was told where the
place was, and he and his minister set out to find it. At last they
came to a shabby house with a broken tin door. Inside a voice
was heard, muffled with weeping. A poor woman opened the
door.

"Shalom, my good woman," they said. "We are thirsty and
tired, and we have been a long way on foot. We would like to
rest awhile. May we have some water, please?"

Meanwhile they looked around the house and saw an infant
lying on straw.

"How old is the baby, my good woman?" asked the king.

"One week old, sir, and I have nothing other than his swaddling
clothes to wrap him up in, so I put him down on the straw." The
woman served her guests with water from a tin and told them
of her hardships, apologizing that she had nothing else to offer
them. The king and his minister were amazed. Could it be that

the husband of the king's daughter would come from this house and be a bastard? "This shall not be!" exclaimed the king to his minister. "This infant must not be the fate of my daughter!" Whereon both of them tried to persuade the mother to sell her infant to them.

"How can I sell my own infant? My life. I suffered so much on his account," wailed the mother. However, the guests urged that with the large sum of the money offered her she would be able to live in greater happiness than with an infant whom she had no money to feed. Both would undoubtedly die of hunger. But if she sold her son, she would probably have more children in the future. Of course, they promised that her son would have a good and happy life.

At last the woman agreed. The guests handed her the money and set off with the infant in their arms. On the way they saw a mill. The king commanded the minister, "Take the infant and throw him on the turning wheel." The minister carried out the king's order, but the infant remained hooked to a nail by his swaddling clothes and did not fall on the mill wheel.

The mill stopped working, and the miller came to see what had happened. He saw the infant and succeeded in removing him from the nail, safe and sound. "I shall bring him up, and he will be a help in my old age," said the miller in his heart. "It is a gift from the Almighty."

Many years went by. One day the king and his minister remembered the infant and the prophecy of the dervish. "What do you think about the child?" the king asked his minister with a triumphant laugh.

"Maybe he is still alive, my king. With God's will, all is possible. There is no escape from fate."

"How absurd! Just listen to what you are saying! Did you not with your own hands throw the infant on the mill wheel?" asked the king.

They decided to visit the mill. They came to the place, and lo! there, beside the miller, a youth was seated. They asked the miller, "Who is this boy?" "My son," replied the miller. They talked to him and questioned him until he disclosed the whole truth. "One day the mill stopped working. I went to see what had happened

and saw an infant hanging by his swaddling clothes on a nail
of the mill wheel. I adopted him as a son because I am old and
have no children of my own."

They both began to persuade the old miller to sell them the
boy for a large sum of money. At last he agreed and went to fetch
the boy. Said the king to his minister, "This time I shall kill him
with my own hands. I shall not entrust you with this mission."

The three of them reached a deserted lane where no one passed.
The king took out his sword and began striking the youth. He
continued striking and knocking him until he was like mincemeat. "Enough! Enough!" called out the minister. "You have
not left a single bone in his body."

They left the boy lying by the roadside and sped back to the
palace.

A famous doctor was living in that town. By chance he was
called out that night on an urgent house visit. He mounted his
horse and set off. When he reached a fork in the road, his horse
halted and refused to go on. The doctor began to beat him, but
to no avail. The horse would not budge from the spot. Said the
doctor to himself, "What can it be? I shall let the horse go his
own way." The horse went along the second narrow lane, and
lo! the doctor saw there the prostrate body of a youth.

The doctor dismounted and examined the youth, looking for
signs of life. After examining the entire body, he found at last
one beating nerve in the heart. He was encouraged and began to
treat the beating nerve, quite forgetting the sick man he had set
out to visit. The treatment took a long time, but at last he succeeded in awakening the youth. Then he put him on a plank and
took him to the hospital.

Time passed, and the youth recovered. He became the doctor's
assistant and lived with him as his adopted son. Days passed;
years went by. One day the king and his minister remembered
the infant and the prophecy of the dervish. With a triumphant
laugh, the king asked the minister, "What do you think about
the infant? Do you still dare to tell me he is alive?" The minister
answered, "My king! With God's will, all is possible. There is no
escape from fate."

They decided to go along the same path where they had left the youth. Before long they came to the town and walked to and fro, interesting themselves in everything. At one place they saw a crowd assembled and asked, "What is happening here?"

The people answered, "An excellent doctor lives here, and people from far and wide come to consult him."

The king and his minister pushed the queue aside and entered. And what did they see? A youth was distributing numbers to the waiting patients, a youth with the looks of the miller's boy. They could not believe their own eyes. Then they saw stitches on his face and body and knew that it was he. They went in to see the doctor and began talking to and questioning him. It became clear that the youth was the same unfortunate boy whom the minister had thrown into the mill wheel and the king had turned into mincemeat. The king and his minister persuaded the doctor to sell the youth for a large sum of money. The king then sent the youth to one of his ministers and gave him a sealed letter which had the following order written in the king's own handwriting, "When this youth arrives, put him to death at once."

The youth took the letter, mounted his horse, and set off. When he arrived at his destination, he found the city gates closed. What was he to do? Miserable one, so weary, hungry, and thirsty! He tethered his horse, put the letter under his head, and lay down to sleep near the walls of the closed city.

That same night the king's daughter had a restless sleep and wandered around her room without finding repose. As she was looking over the balcony, her eyes fell on the man sleeping by the walls of the city. The moon lit up his face. How beautiful he was! "What is the young man doing there? Why is he lying in the open? she thought to herself. Suddenly she beheld the letter underneath his head. She called out to her attendants, "Is there one among you willing to climb down a rope, approach the sleeping youth, hand me the letter under his head, and replace it without awakening him? If one of you can do this, I shall set her free at once."

An attendant called out, "I will go down!" And she climbed down the rope, took the letter from under the young man's head, and brought it to the princess.

The king's daughter read the letter and was very surprised at her father. Fool that he was! Such a handsome young man! Fancy wanting to have him killed! Immediately she took the letter and put another in its place, with the words, "On this young man's arrival, take him at once to my daughter!" She signed the letter with the king's stamp, sealed it with the king's seal, and asked her attendant to place it under the young man's head.

Early the following morning, when the city gates were opened, the young man was welcomed with joy. The inhabitants of the city arranged a magnificent wedding, befitting a king.

During the next three years, the king was at war and did not visit the city. In the meantime three children were born to the king's daughter and the young man.

At last the war was over and won. One day a letter arrived with the news that the king, his ministers, and his army were about to return to the city and to celebrate the victory. The king's daughter decided to arrange a splendid reception. First there was a procession and at the head, of course, were her husband and the king's grandchildren. When the king and his followers approached the city, the king asked his minister to look through his field glasses and see if his citizens had come out to welcome him. His minister looked and exclaimed, "I see a large crowd, but it is not ours!" After a short time the minister looked again and exclaimed, "What a crowd!" As the procession drew nearer he saw three children riding ahead, aged one year, two years, and three years.

"Who are these children? Why are they leading the procession?" thought the king and his ministers. When the two parties were face to face, the king heard his daughter say to her husband, "Take the hand of your father-in-law and kiss it." Then she turned to the children and said, "This is your grandfather, my children."

The vizier, who acted as the king's deputy in his absence, told of the letter they received.

"What letter? What are you talking about?" wondered the king and rushed out to question his daughter.

She related all that had happened and all she had done. The king said to his minister, "Now I see and understand that everything I did was of no use. Nothing has changed my daughter's fate or the prophecy of the dervish. With God's will all is possible. There is no escape from fate."

The king embraced his daughter and appointed his son-in-law as his heir.

·50·   The Box with Bones

IFA 422. Recorded in 1958 by Ozer Pipe, a member of the collective settlement Gat, from David Fishbein, aged fifty, of Sokolov, Poland, who came to Israel from São Paulo, Brazil, where he lived for seven years after World War II.

The text combines Type 506, The Rescued Princess, episodes I, "The Grateful Dead Man," and V, "The Dividing in Halves," and Type 507C, The Serpent Maiden. For Palestinian-Arab analogues of this combination, see H. Schmidt-P. Kahle, I, 85–99, and for a Lower Euphrates-Arabic version, see C. G. Campbell, Tales from the Arab Tribes, p. 11. Jewish versions are given in A. S. Rappoport, The Folklore of the Jews, pp. 132–36; M. Gaster, Studies and Texts, II, 1071–75. An extensive bibliography of Hebrew and European versions can be found in M. Gaster, The Exempla of the Rabbis, Nos. 334, 439, 440; and cf. J. Bolte-G. Polívka, III, 494. Two monographs are devoted to this tale-complex: G. H. Gerould, The Grateful Dead (London, 1908), and S. Liljeblad, Die Tobiasgeschichte und andere Märchen mit Toten Helfen (Lund, 1927). The apocryphal Book of Tobit, written between the fourth and the second centuries B.C., was the first Hebrew literary treatment of this tale type.

See also M. Grunwald, No. 17 (Sephardic-Jewish), E. S. Druzhinina, Kurdish Tales, No. 10 (Kurdish), and M. N. Kabirov-V. F. Shahmatov, No. 26 (Uigur).

• THERE ONCE lived a very rich couple. They had an only son who was not too bright. When he grew up, the mother asked her husband, the merchant, to look out for the boy and find him a trade.

"Good," the husband agreed and sent his son to a fair in one of the towns near the capital. Arriving at the fair, the son saw someone selling pipes; children gathered round the pipe-seller, grabbing them out of his hand, so eager were they to buy them. The son said in his heart, "I shall buy a box full of pipes, and on my return home I shall make a fortune." So he bought a box of pipes and returned home. When he opened the box, what did he find? All the pipes were broken.

Said his father, the merchant, to his wife, "I could have told you that would happen."

Now let us leave the rich merchant, his wife, and his son, and go to another place where a Jew was living on a farm leased from a gentile landlord. This Jew lost a large sum of money in business, and he still had a big debt to settle with his landlord. What did the landlord do? He decided to keep the Jew in a store-room and to starve him to death if he still refused to pay the debt. The Jew died in captivity, whereupon the landlord collected his bones in a box and ordered one of his servants to sell it at the fair.

In the meantime the rich merchant's wife once again asked her husband to fix up her son in business. Again the father took no notice of her pleading. But what does one not do for peace in a family? The father agreed, and once again the son was sent to the fair. He walked to and fro and saw a peasant crying out his wares in a loud voice, "A box of Jewish bones for sale! A box of Jewish bones for sale!"

Of course, these were the bones of the poor Jewish farmer who had passed away in captivity. The boy did not think twice and bought the bones. With the help of the burial society he brought the bones to a Jewish cemetery and buried them there. Then he returned home, saying to his father, "I have done a good deed. I bought Jewish bones and buried them in the Jewish cemetery."

That night in a dream, a man appeared before the rich merchant and bade him, "If you want your son to succeed, do as I tell you. Rinse your hands when you wake up in the morning and then leave the house. Suggest to the first Jew you meet on your way that he become your son's partner and go with him to the fair. You will see what a successful partnership this will be."

In the morning the father arose with a light heart and said to himself, "Dreams are bubbles."

Yet the same man appeared to him once again the next night in his sleep and on the third night too. The following morning the merchant did as the man in the dream advised him. He rinsed his hands and then left his house. And lo! he saw a Jew with a staff in his hand and a bag on his shoulders. He approached him: "Whither?"

"To the fair."

"Why must you go on foot?" asked the merchant. "Be my son's partner, and you will get a cart drawn by horses. It will be better for both of you."

The wayfarer agreed. And so it was. The horses were harnessed to the cart, and the two partners went on their way with other merchants. They went on until they found themselves in a dense forest. Then the merchant's son and his partner left the others and drove along till they came to a sturdy tree. There they stopped, and the partner got out of the cart, saying to the merchant's son, "Stay here till I come." Then he set off in the direction of a small house. He approached it, and looking through a chink in the walls, he saw thieves busy inside. In one of the corners there were hands, legs, and heads, as well as silver and precious stones, piled up.

He entered the house and said, "I am one of your trade. Let us become partners. The merchants, who are on their way here, have with them rich treasures of gold. If you send me your men one by one, we shall get rid of all the merchants."

One by one the robbers came to him, and one by one the partner beheaded them. Then he returned to the merchant's son, saying, "Now let us be off!"

They rode to the robbers' den, filled a jar with gold and precious stones, and set off on their way.

In the meantime the Sabbath approached, and they arrived at an inn owned by a Jew. There they asked the innkeeper to put them up for the night.

"I have no food," the innkeeper informed them.

"Take three rubles, and prepare everything for the Sabbath," the partners proposed.

So they stayed with the Jew. On Friday night, when they sat down for supper, they saw that their host was serving food to a hand, stretched out through a half-closed door. And so it happened at every meal. It is not customary to ask questions on Sabbath, so they kept quiet, but on Saturday evening they asked the innkeeper, "Tell us, please, whose hand was that stretching out for food at mealtimes?"

The host answered, "Even if you fill my house with silver and gold, I shall never reveal this secret."

But they did not stop inquiring and nagging until he answered, "That is my daughter. Three times she was wedded, and on each wedding night her husband died."

Said the partner, "Never mind; I have a husband for your daughter."

"What are you thinking of? He will surely die," exclaimed the host in fear.

"Do not worry. Nothing will happen to him," replied the partner, and he kept on repeating his offer until the innkeeper agreed to his daughter's marriage with the merchant's son.

They fixed a date for the wedding and when it drew near, the innkeeper said to his wife, "Buy candles because soon there will be another death in this house." The wife bought candles, and both of them began to lament the death to be.

After the wedding ceremony the partner said to the merchant's son, "Now is the time for us to part and to divide all our possessions." So they began dividing their treasures: "A ring for you and a ring for me, silver for you and silver for me, gold for you and gold for me." So they continued until everything had been divided between them.

Then said the partner, "Now we shall divide your bride, half for me and half for you."

"How can we?" shouted the merchant's son. "How can one divide a woman into two? Either I pay you for your share or you take her for yourself!"

But the partner did not agree. "We shall cut her into two," he insisted. Then he tied her to a tree, took out a shiny knife and got ready to sever the girl. But before he had time to do so, a big frightened snake popped out of the girl's mouth, and the partner cut it into pieces.

In the morning the bride's parents were overcome with joy when they saw their daughter safe and sound. On the same day the partner approached the merchant's son and said to him, "Go home and live a life of happiness and contentment. And tell your father that your partner is no other than the Jew who appeared three times in his dreams. And he is the very Jew whose bones you bought and buried in the Jewish cemetery. Thus I have repaid you for your good deed."

The partner finished speaking and disappeared.

• 51 •   The Queen Who Was a Witch

IFA 6. Recorded by Elisheva Schoenfeld in Affula in 1956 from Mordechai "Marko" Litsi, a merchant, born in Adrianople, Turkey, and brought up in Saloniki, Greece.

This text belongs to Type 449, The Tsar's Dog (Sidi Numan). Eight Turkish variants of Type 449 are listed in W. Eberhard-P. N. Boratav, No. 204, "Die Geschichte des Sinan Pascha (III)." The Motifs D141, "Transformation: man to dog," D154.1, "Transformation: man to dove," D132, "Transformation: man to ass," and D766.1, "Disenchantmant by bathing (immersing) in water," are well known in Jewish-Mediterranean folktales. The Negro as lover is reminiscent of the black slave in The Thousand and One Nights. Cf. W. Eberhard- P. N. Boratav, Index, s.v. "Neger," p. 471. A similar tale from Ossetia (Caucasus area) is recorded in A. H. Bjazirov, No. 10.

• MANY YEARS AGO there lived a king who was beloved by all his people. He was puzzled by one thing—every night his wife became ill, while in the day she was always well. At that time it was the custom for the king to ask the queen for permission to come to her. But the queen was always ill at night.

The king wanted to find out more about her illness. So early one evening he went stealthily to her room and stood before her door. He saw her leave the room quietly, take her white horse from the courtyard, and then ride beyond the town. The king decided to follow her. Before long she came to an open field where she halted in front of a big stone and dismounted from her horse. She intoned a word, and—behold—the stone rolled aside revealing a door. The queen went through the door and disappeared below the ground. The king followed her, taking care not to be seen. Suddenly they came to a magnificent palace. The queen entered the first hall, whereupon a Negro approached her. The two of them embraced, kissed, and made love to each other. Then the queen left and returned to the palace. At that moment the king jumped out of his hiding place, unsheathed his sword, and beheaded the Negro. Then he took the Negro's head to the palace, put it on a plate and in the morning brought it into the queen's room.

When the queen saw the head of her lover, she pricked the king with a pin, saying, "Be a dog from now on!" Immediately the king was transformed into a dog, and the queen ordered her guards to throw him out into the street.

All day long the dog wandered about in the streets without finding food. Passers-by took pity on him and threw him crumbs, but the dog was used to clean food served on a plate, so he began to feel hungry and weary. In the evening he found himself outside a grain merchant's shop. Just then the merchant's son came out into the street and taking pity on the hungry dog handed him a slice of bread. The dog began to show signs of affection for the boy, so he took him home and looked after him.

One day the merchant asked his son, "Where is all the money your are earning in the shop? Are you spending it on food for the dog? That is very foolish! You had better turn out the dog and spend the money on something more useful."

When the dog heard the merchant's words, he began to jump up and down on one of the shelves. The merchant wondered what he wanted. A box full of coins is what he saw on the shelf, and he realized that this was his son's money. So the dog continued to live at the home of the grain merchant.

The merchant also had a daughter. One day she came home from school with a paper reporting the disappearance of the king, whose whereabouts were unknown. The merchant and his children had been wondering for a long time about the dog's unusual intelligence and his love for cleanliness. Suddenly the daughter burst out, "I know! The dog is nobody else but the king! We will wash him and return him to the palace." She prepared a hot bath and scrubbed the dog with soap, and then before she had even finished washing him, the king himself stood before her. He embraced the girl and went back to the palace, carrying in his heart a great hatred for the queen.

The queen was already aware of these happenings. She took various kinds of grasses and burned them, so that a heavy smoke arose and was carried by the wind across the face of the returning king. The minute he breathed in the smoke he forgot his hatred, and with a happy, carefree heart he approached the queen.

But alas! Suddenly he saw the head of the Negro in the cupboard and broke out in anger, "Is the Negro still here?"

The queen again pricked the king's face with a pin, saying, "Be a dove from now on!"

The king turned into a dove and flew to the house of his friend, the merchant, and his children. Fortunately for him, when he arrived the young daughter was washing clothes. The dove plunged into the hot soapy water and once again returned to his real form, whereupon the girl gave him a pin saying, "Prick your wife with this pin, and turn her into any animal you wish."

The king thanked her, took the pin, and returned to the palace. Straight away he went to the queen's room, pricked her with the pin, and said, "Be a donkey from now on!" And so it was. The queen turned into a she-donkey and was put into the stable by the guards.

One day the king called his chief builder and ordered him, "Build me another palace on that hill, opposite my palace. I know it is difficult to carry building materials to such a height, but this she-donkey will help you. She is very strong and will carry all the materials you need to the hill."

So the donkey did all the hard work. After a few months she could no longer stand on her feet, and she finally tumbled over and died.

·52· The Only Daughter of Noah the Righteous

IFA 660. Recorded by Sara Ilani, a kindergarten teacher, from a Sephardic-Jewish woman.

Motif A1371.3, "Bad women from transformed hog and goose," refers to J. Balys, Motif-Index of Lithuanian Narrative Folk-Lore, No. 411 (The Three Brides: the Girl, the Sow and the Mare), a close parallel. Other versions, collected from Palestinian Arabs, are given in J. E. Hanauer, Folk-Lore of the Holy Land, pp. 16–17, and Abu Naaman, On the Way to the Land of Happiness, No. 20 (Hebrew). The most important general motif here is "Suitor tests" (H310–H359), e.g., H359.2, "Suitor test: clearing land." Also present in this tale are Motifs B651.4, "Marriage to dog in human form," D332.1, "Transformation: ass (donkey) to person," and D341.1, "Transformation: bitches to women."

Adam and Mohammed are substituted for Noah in other recorded IFA versions of this popular legend.

• NOAH THE RIGHTEOUS had three sons and an only daughter who was renowned for her beauty, wisdom, and goodness. In the whole world she had no equal. Suitors came from the far corners of the earth to ask for her hand in marriage.

One day, Noah was standing at the threshold of his tent, and he saw a handsome young man coming from the east, riding on a white horse. He dismounted and said, "Noah, O Righteous One! I have heard much of your fair daughter, her wisdom and goodness, and I beg for her hand in marriage."

The Righteous One replied, "My son, have you already planted your vineyard?"

The young man was silent, and Noah continued, "It is not the custom in our place to marry off a daughter to a man who has not yet planted his vineyard. Plant your vineyard and then come back, and we will talk about it again."

The young man jumped on his white horse and rode towards the east. And he kept the words of the Righteous One in his heart.

One day, Noah was standing at the threshold of his tent, and he saw a handsome young man coming from the west, riding on a black horse. He dismounted and said, "Noah, O Righteous One! I have heard so much of your fair daughter, her wisdom and goodness, and I desire to make her my wife."

The Righteous One asked, "Tell me, my son. Have you already planted your vineyard?"

"Yes, O Righteous One!" said the man, "my vineyard is already planted."

Noah inquired, "Tell me, my son, have you already built a home to dwell in?"

The young man kept quiet and did not reply. Noah continued, "It is not the custom, in our place, to marry off a daughter to a man who has not built his home. Build your home and then come back, and we will talk it over again."

The young man jumped on his black horse and rode towards the west. And the words of the Righteous One were kept in his heart.

One day Noah was standing at the threshold of his tent, and he saw a handsome young man coming from the south, riding on a brown horse. He dismounted and said, "O Righteous One! I have heard so much of your fair daughter, her wisdom and goodness. I should like to be the most humble member in your family."

Noah asked, "Tell me, my son. Have you already planted your vineyard?"

"Yes, O Righteous One! My vineyard is planted."

Noah continued to ask, "My son, have you built a house?"

"Yes," answered the young man, "I have built a house."

Noah was pleased with the young man and gave him his daughter in marriage. Great was the joy, which lasted seven days and seven nights. And on the eighth day the young man lifted Noah's daughter on his brown horse and rode to his home in the south.

One day Noah was standing on the threshold of his tent, and he saw coming from the east the young man on the white horse, who bore the following tidings, "My vineyard is planted, my house is built."

Noah regretted that he had no other daughter and was not able to keep his promise. Suddenly he saw that the she-donkey outside his tent had been transformed into a beautiful woman. He understood that the Almighty did not wish the Righteous to be sorrowful, and the change was a sign from heaven. So Noah gave the young man the beautiful woman. Great was the rejoicing, which lasted seven days and seven nights. And on the eighth day the young man lifted his bride on his white horse and set out for his home in the east.

One day Noah was standing at the threshold of his tent, and he saw coming from the west the handsome young man on the black horse, who bore the following tidings, "My vineyard is planted and my house is built."

Noah regretted that he had no daughter to give the young man and was unable to keep his promise. Suddenly he saw that the bitch outside his tent had been transformed into a beautiful woman. He understood that the Almighty did not want the Righteous to be sorrowful and had given a sign from heaven. So Noah gave the beautiful woman to the young man. Great was the rejoicing, which lasted seven days and seven nights, and on the eighth day the young man lifted his wife on his black horse and set out for his home in the west.

And since then, until today, there have been three kinds of women. There are stupid, lazy, and obstinate women, like an ass; for them the lash is good. There are bad, bickering, and shouting women, like a bitch; and for them the stick is good. But happy is the man blessed with a clever, quiet, and diligent woman. She is the true daughter of Noah the Righteous One.

Part VII
Heroes and Heroines

·53· Who Cured the Princess?

IFA 464. Recorded by Moshe Kaplan, as heard from a Polish rabbi.

Type 653A, The Rarest Thing in the World. For other Jewish tales containing Motif H346, "Princess given to man who can heal her," see M. Gaster, The Exempla of the Rabbis, No. 330; Gaster (ed.), The Ma'aseh Book, No. 224; and A. D. L. Palacin, No. 129. Type 653A has come to the New World in the Spanish and Negro traditions. Fourteen Turkish examples of Type 653, the parent tale of The Four Skilful Brothers, are cited in W. Eberhard–P. N. Boratav, No. 291, "Das geheilte Mädchen." See also A. H. Bjazirov, No. 14 (from Ossetia); E. S. Druzhinina, No. 10 (from Kurdistan); and M. I. Shewerdin, Vol. I, No. 54 (from Uzbekistan).

Three brief, well-told variants from Gullah Negroes are given by E. C. Parsons in Folk-Lore of the Sea Islands, South Carolina, *(Memoirs of the American Folklore Society, XVI [1923]), No. 66 ("Trackwell, Divewell, Breathewell"), pp. 75–76. In her introduction (p. xvii), Parsons comments on the African analogues and character of this tale.*

• MANY YEARS AGO there were three brothers whose father died leaving them practically penniless. They had no means of livelihood, so they decided to go out into the big world, each one on a different path, and to meet again in ten years, each bringing with him something remarkable acquired during his travels.

The brothers parted, and each wandered in a different corner of the world. The eldest brother went to America, and after roaming about for some time, he settled in the United States. There was great development in technology and industry at that time, so after doing this, that, and the other, the brother started to construct airplanes. At last he succeeded in making a small, swift three-passenger plane that could soar in the clouds at a very high speed.

The second brother went to Asia. He suffered many hardships and misfortunes and then reached India. He wandered among the different tribes there, becoming familiar with their ways of life and languages, and in no time he won their friendship. He kept company with magicians and fakirs, and so it was that once he came across a fakir with something quite unique—a magic mirror that revealed what was going on in far-off lands. How the brother entreated and begged the fakir for the mirror! How many gifts he offered in exchange for it! Then at last the fakir gave in to the brother's whim, and the magic mirror was his.

The youngest brother went to Africa and wandered in every corner of the Black Continent until he became black-skinned. Wherever he went, he won the friendship of the wild and semi-wild African tribes. He learned their languages and felt like one amongst them. Once he came to an isolated place inhabited by a wild tribe and succeeded in winning the trust and friendship of the chief. One day he came across a strange apple tree such as he had never seen before. The tribesmen guarded this tree by day and by night and did not give anyone, not even their own comrades, the right to approach. The youngest brother began to wonder about the value of this tree and why it was so carefully guarded. At last it came to his ears that this was an exceptional tree and the only one of its kind in the whole of Africa. Anyone who was sick and tasted apples from this tree recovered immediately and became immune from every malady.

The youngest brother began to plan how he could find a way to pluck one of these rare apples from the tree, but all his tricks and strategies were unsuccessful. Once he managed to obtain a string of colored beads, and he showed them to the head watchman, who began examining the necklace. The other watchmen also could not take their eyes off the beads, and while they were gazing at them, the third brother grasped his chance and plucked an apple from the tree, hiding it amongst his belongings. Then he went off, leaving the beads with one of the watchmen.

When he was far away, he saw there was no longer any danger, and then he remembered that the time was drawing near for the meeting with his brothers, and he set off for the trysting place.

The three brothers welcomed each other with warmth and affection, for it was ten long years since they had met. One by one they related their adventures and displayed their treasures: the speedy airplane, the magic mirror, and the healing apple. Each one boasted that his possession was beyond compare, so at last they decided to test out the three treasures to see which of them was finest.

The second brother looked through his magic mirror, and in the capital of a faraway land he saw great confusion at the king's palace. Doctors scurried to and fro, and everyone was very sad. The king's only daughter was dangerously ill, and her father was desperate about her. He asked the doctors to do their best to save her, but it was beyond their power.

The eldest brother then suggested flying by plane to the far-off kingdom in order to cure the king's daughter with the healing apple. So it was that the three brothers were soon in the air, flying on their way to the sick princess. After a few hours they reached the capital. As soon as they arrived, they went to the king's palace and announced, "We have the power to save the king's daughter."

The king warned them, "If you do not keep your promise, you will be hanged. However, if you succeed in curing my daughter, I will give her to one of you in marriage, and the one who is chosen will inherit my throne, while his brothers will serve him as ministers."

The youngest brother went to the king's sick daughter and gave her the apple to taste. She immediately felt better and after an hour even began to speak. Imagine how excited the king was when he heard her voice! After a few hours she sat up in bed and asked for food. In the evening she arose from her bed, and the next day she was sound and healthy. The joy of the king and his ministers knew no bounds. The king proclaimed that he would fulfil his promise to the three brothers, and he arranged a magnificent party in their honor. Then he went to his daughter and told her to choose a husband amongst the brothers, according to her heart's desire. But the brothers were each so handsome, strong, and clever that she was unable to make up her mind whom to choose. So she proposed that the three brothers should decide themselves. They began to discuss the matter together, and each one was keen to win the king's fair daughter. The eldest son said, "If it was not for my plane we would never have reached the capital in time, and what would have been the use of the healing apple if we had arrived too late?"

The second son said, "Without my magic mirror we would not have known about the princess and her illness."

The youngest brother protested, "Without my apple the princess would never have been cured; neither the swift plane nor the magic mirror would have helped her."

The brothers could not decide who should be chosen, so they went to the king and asked him to make the choice. The king listened to their story, and he too was not able to come to a decision, so he turned to his Jewish adviser, renowned throughout the land for his great wisdom. The adviser heard their story and turning to the eldest brother said, "Was anything missing from your plane after your journey?"

"No," answered the eldest brother. The adviser put the same question to the second brother. But again "No" was the answer. "My magic mirror remained intact."

Finally, the adviser asked the youngest brother the same question.

"Yes, a portion of the apple is missing, the piece eaten by the princess."

"In that case the great prize is due to you," declared the adviser.

The king, his daughter, the princess, and the three brothers agreed that the adviser's decision was a just one. A splendid wedding was arranged and there was joy and happiness in the state. The new king appointed his two brothers as his trusty ministers, and they chose brides from the king's family.

Stories of the exploits of the brothers in different continents, of their wonderful possessions, and of the wisdom of the Jewish adviser are told from generation to generation until this very day.

· 54 · The Hunter and the King's Fair Daughter

IFA 56. Recorded by Elisheva Schoenfeld in Affula in 1956 from Aaron Tsadok, a merchant, born in Radna, central Yemen.

Type 513C, The Son of the Hunter, somewhat expanded and altered from the archetype. Many motifs (e.g., the shed, a demon with long ears) are local and point toward a local Arabic form of the tale. This tale type is reported only from the Mediterranean and Moslem cultural areas. See M. I. Shewerdin, Vol. II, No. 75 (central Asia), and C. G. Campbell, Told in the Market Place, pp. 48–57.

• MANY YEARS AGO there lived a hunter and his wife. They did not have any children and this made them very sad because they were already old. One day a soothsayer came, and they told him of their sorrow. He said to them, "In due time, a child will be born to you."

"But we are old people," said the hunter in astonishment. "My wife can no longer give birth, and I can no longer beget a son."

"Indeed, you will give birth to a son," said the soothsayer. "Just one thing; never disclose his father's craft to him, or many hardships will befall him." The soothsayer finished speaking to the hunter and his wife and then disappeared from sight.

In due course, a son was born. The old people were very happy and reared him with love. Never did they reveal his father's craft.

The son grew up, and after a time his father died. One day the son asked his mother, "Tell me, Mother, what did my father do? What was his craft?"

"Your father was a forester, my son," answered his mother.

The son got up, placed an ax on his shoulder, and went to the forest to fell trees. Before long he realized that the work did not appeal to him, and he did not have the strength to carry on. One day he sat by the wayside and wept bitter tears. A man passed, saw him weeping, and said, "What is it, my son? Why are you weeping?"

The young man answered, "My father was a forester, yet this work does not make me happy, and I have no strength to do it. That is why I am weeping."

"Your father was not a forester, he was a hunter," said the passer-by, "and that is why you have no pleasure in cutting trees. Go home and vex your mother until she curses you, and then you will realize that what I have told you is correct."

The boy went home and began to vex his mother until she said to him, "Hunter, son of hunter! Why do you anger me?" She continued talking without heeding the words she uttered. So it was revealed to the boy that his father was a hunter; and the words of the man in the forest had been true. Whereupon the boy took a bow and arrows and went off to hunt.

One day he caught a golden bird in the forest, and he thought in his heart: "What a pity to kill such a beautiful bird; I shall sell it." He did not know the value of the bird so he went to the market and offered the bird for sale in a shop. The shopkeeper did not have enough money to buy the bird, so the boy went to a second shop and then to a third one. He always heard the same answer: "We have not enough money." At last he took the bird home with him. By this time, rumors of the golden bird had spread throughout the kingdom and had also reached the ears of the sultan's vizier, a blind Jew. He appeared before the sultan and said, "Your majesty, many treasures are in your coffers, but one thing is lacking, a golden bird."

The sultan asked him, "Where can I seek such a bird?" The vizier answered, "In your town there lives a hunter, and he has such a bird."

The sultan gave an order for the hunter to appear before him, and when he came, the sultan said to him, "I have heard that you have a golden bird. Bring it to me, and you will be paid your due; if not, you will be beheaded." The hunter thought for a moment and then asked for a day's grace in order to retrieve the golden bird from a buyer. The sultan agreed, and the next day the hunter brought the bird to the palace, whereupon the sultan weighed out gold for the hunter according to the bird's weight.

After a few days the vizier once again appeared before the sultan. "Your majesty," he began, "you have everything in your coffers, except a bowl of God." This time, too, the sultan paid close attention to the vizier's words and asked him, "Who can find me such a bowl?"

"There is no one except the hunter who brought the golden bird here," answered the vizier.

For the second time the sultan ordered the vizier to fetch the hunter. When he arrived, the sultan said to him, "I have heard that you have the bowl of God. Bring it to me, and you will be paid your due; and if not, you will be beheaded." The hunter begged for time to think about the matter and said, "Within three days I shall bring you an answer." The sultan agreed, and the hunter went to the desert. When the day turned into night, the hunter made his bed at the foot of a high mountain near the opening of a cave. At midnight the hunter awoke and saw before him a *shed* with very long ears. One ear served him as a mattress and the other as a blanket. He challenged the hunter to a sword duel.

"Wait! Before we begin to fight," called out the hunter, "I have something to tell you. So listen to me!" This aroused the curiosity of the *shed*. "What have you to tell me?" he asked.

"The sultan gave me an order to bring him the bowl of God or he will behead me," said the hunter.

"If so, you have a hard task in front of you, and you will have to save your strength. The bowl of God is in the seventh kingdom in the palace of the king of *shedim*. Only once a week, on Sabbath, a hundred soldiers wearing swords take out the bowl and carry it through the streets of the city. I am ready to help you if you do everything I tell you. There are two alternatives. If we are successful, we will carry away the bowl; if not, both of us will perish."

The hunter answered, "I will listen to you." Thereupon the devil pulled out a hair from his head, gave it to him, and departed with the following words: "Leave this place in the morning, and go on until you are so tired that you feel yourself neither in heaven nor on earth. Then burn my hair, and I will come for help."

At sunrise, the hunter got up and set out on his way. He went on and on, until he was so tired that he felt himself neither in heaven nor on earth. Then he took out the hair, burned it, and the *shed* stood in front of him. The *shed* put the hunter on his shoulders and soared far up into the sky. He flew and flew till he reached the border of the seventh kingdom. Then he put the hunter on the ground and said to him: "Wait here till Sabbath. Then enter the town, walk around, and mingle with the onlookers at the procession of the bowl of God. When the bowl passes in front of you, ask to touch it. Clutch hold of it, and I will come to help you."

"I shall do what you have told me," promised the hunter. And he sat at the border of the seventh kingdom and waited for the Sabbath to come.

On the Sabbath morning, the hunter entered the town and mingled with the crowds as if he were one of them. Then he took a place next to the king. From far off he could already see the big procession coming closer to him. But where was the bowl of God? Then when the parade was very close, he saw one hundred soldiers raising their swords so that the bowl would not blind the people's eyes. "Let me touch the bowl," begged the hunter when the procession approached. One of the soldiers moved aside, and the hunter grabbed the bowl in both of his hands. At that moment a cloud covered the sun. And who was the cloud? The *shed* himself. He dropped like a plane to the ground, caught hold of the bowl, and flew with the hunter to the heavens. 'Way up they soared till they could no longer be seen from the ground except as a tiny speck in the sky. The soldiers had no way of chasing the thieves. The hunter and the *shed* flew until they reached the cave, whereupon the hunter sent word to the sultan of his arrival with the bowl of God and requested him to take it in splendor to the capital. The sultan arrived with all his court, and eleven hundred soldiers bore the bowl on their shoulders. They carried it from the desert to the city and from there to the king's palace.

Meanwhile the *shed* parted from the hunter. "Take this hair, and burn it when you need me," he said and disappeared from the hunter's sight.

The blind vizier did not leave the sultan in peace. "Your majesty," he said to him one day. "You have everything in your palace except one thing: the fair daughter of Sinsin."

Again the sultan listened to the vizier's words and said, "And who will find her and bring her to me?"

"There is no one except the hunter who found and brought you the golden bird and the bowl of God."

The sultan ordered one of his bodyguards to fetch the hunter, and when he appeared, the king said to him, "Bring me Sinsin's fair daughter or you will be beheaded."

The hunter had no other course but to obey the sultan. He went home and divided his money in two piles. He gave one of them to his mother in case he should not return and took the other one to the market to buy camels and flour. Then he set out to search for Sinsin's fair daughter. On the way huge ants bore down upon the camels and dug deep into the flour. And who were these huge ants? No other than *shedim!* And they ate all the flour. After this meal the king of the ants, who was a *shed,* said to the hunter, "Fellow creature! We were very hungry, and you helped us to still our hunger. As a reward I give you some of my hairs; burn them in the hour of need and danger, and we shall come to your aid." And in the twinkling of an eye, he disappeared.

The hunter continued on his way until he was very tired, and he felt himself neither in heaven nor on earth. Then he took from his pocket a hair of his first friend, the long-eared *shed,* and burned it. Immediately the *shed* appeared before him and asked, "What is your wish, sir?"

"The sultan sent me to fetch Sinsin's fair daughter. I do not know how to find his country, and I have become so weary that my legs will scarcely carry me any more."

"That is a most difficult mission for you, sir," said the *shed.* "Ninety-nine young men have already lost their lives for her sake. I warn you; maybe you too will be killed."

"The sultan will behead me if I do not fetch her, so I must try my luck. If I do not, I shall die in any case."

The long-eared *shed* picked up the hunter on his shoulders, ascended to the heavens, and flew to Sinsin's country. He dropped the hunter on the palace roof and disappeared. The hunter looked around. There were ninety-nine men strung up on ropes. "Surely, they were the suitors who had tried to win Sinsin's daughter without success," he meditated to himself.

The hunter climbed down from the roof and walked into the garden of the palace. There in the garden he came across King Sinsin.

"Good evening, father!" he called to him.

"I am not your father," answered the king.

"Good evening, uncle!"

"I am not your uncle! What is your wish?" asked the king.

"It is my wish to win your fair daughter for a wife, your majesty." The hunter did not disclose that he had come as the sultan's envoy because he thought King Sinsin would throw him out or kill him on the spot.

The king advised him, "Do not mix yourself up in this business. Here are ninety-nine dead men who were killed on that account. You are dear to me, and I do not want you to be the hundredth sacrifice."

The hunter answered, "Whatever will be, I shall try my luck; whether I shall take my place as the hundredth man or be preferred and chosen, fate will decide."

King Sinsin sighed and said, "You have two tasks before you tonight! First, empty all the reservoirs and vessels in my country. Then take a hundred sacks of rich maize and corn mixed together and sort out the different grains. If you accomplish these two tasks, I shall give you my fair daughter. If not, you will be the hundredth man to be hanged."

They parted as it was already evening, and the king retired for the night. The hunter took the second hair from his pocket and burned it. In a trice the long-eared *shed* stood before him. "What is your wish, sir?"

"My task is to empty the water from all the reservoirs and vessels of the kingdom."

The *shed* immediately emptied the water from all the reservoirs and vessels. In the meantime the hunter also burned one of the ant-king's hairs.

"What is your wish?" asked the ant-king, appearing before the hunter.

"I have to sort out rice, maize, and corn mixed together in a hundred sacks. This is the task King Sinsin set me."

Immediately the ant-king called his huge ants, and in no time they sorted the grain.

In the morning there was a great tumult in the town. "We have no water! Our children are thirsty! Our fields are dry! Our cattle are parched with thirst! Give us water! Water!" the people cried. The king looked out of the window and saw an immense crowd gathered in the court. He immediately called the hunter, "I see you have been successful." Afterward both of them went together to the storeroom where the sorted sacks were piled up. "You also performed this task well. But before I give you my daughter you will have to put back the water in the reservoirs and vessels, otherwise my citizens will die of thirst."

The hunter requested that two oxen be brought before him and killed before his eyes. When they had been killed, he took from his pocket the third hair of the long-eared *shed* and burned it. Instantly the *shed* appeared and, in the twinkling of an eye, put all the water back into the reservoirs and vessels.

The wedding of King Sinsin's fair daughter and the hunter was joyously celebrated, and the bridegroom remained in the palace for another month. During all this time, he did not touch the king's daughter because she was betrothed to the sultan in his native land. But King Sinsin's daughter and the hunter loved each other dearly. At the month's end the hunter burned another hair of the ant-king, and when he appeared, the hunter requested: "Take me and King Sinsin's daughter back to my homeland!" And with the fair daughter of King Sinsin on his back, the ant-king soared away up into the heavens and flew to the sultan's country.

Before they parted from each other the couple asked advice from the ant-king, "We are in love with each other, but King Sinsin's daughter is betrothed to the sultan. What are we to do?"

The *shed* answered, "Sinsin's daughter must remain for a month in the sultan's palace. If by then she still loves you, she should kill the sultan and marry you." The ant-king finished his words and disappeared.

Sinsin's fair daughter informed the sultan of her arrival in his country. She agreed to go to his palace on condition that he would have an ox and a blind Jew killed before her eyes. The sultan looked around his entire kingdom for a blind Jew, but he found no one except his vizier. At last he decided to sacrifice him so as to fulfil the request of King Sinsin's fair daughter.

Meanwhile the hunter was waiting in the desert near the entry of the cave. Thirty days passed and Sinsin's fair daughter still loved only the hunter and not the sultan. One day she put poison in the king's wine. He drank it and died. Then Sinsin's fair daughter called her beloved hunter to marry her. The sultan had left no heir, and the citizens of the town turned to the hunter and invited him to succeed the sultan.

So the hunter became sultan. He ruled justly and righteously together with Sinson's fair daughter. They lived in happiness and peace till the end of their days.

•*55*• *The Pupil Who Excelled His Master*

IFA 322. Recorded by M. Ohel from Menahem Mevorakh, born in Tripoli, Libya.

Type 325, The Magician and His Pupil, *and Grimm's tale No. 68, "The Swindler and His Master," a world-famous story, containing Motif D615.2, "Transformation combat." Also present is the popular Motif C611, "Forbidden chamber." Thirty-six Turkish texts are listed in W. Eberhard–P. N. Boratav, No. 169, "Das Ali Cengiz-Spiel." French, Spanish, and Negro examples are known in North America.*

There are many versions of this tale in IFA. For Jewish texts from eastern Europe, see Y. L. Cahan (1931), No. 15, and Cahan (1940), No. 26. C. G. Campbell collected an Arab variant, in From Town and Tribe, *pp. 81–89. For the Caucasus area, see S. Britajev-K. Kasbekov, No. 10 (Ossetia); H. S. Bgazhba, No. 10 (Abkhazia); and E. S. Druzhinina, No. 3 (Kurdistan). Three examples from central Asia are given in M. I. Shewerdin, Vol. I, No. 47, and Vol. II, Nos. 68, 119.*

• THIS IS the story of a boy who was always delving into all kinds of ideas and inventions. He had an old mother, but he was unable to provide for her because he was always wrapped up in his dreams. So his mother never stopped weeping, and he reproached her bitterly.

One day he begged his mother to go to the governor and tell

him that her son wished to woo his daughter. At first his mother was unwilling to go, but her son pleaded until at last she went.

She arrived at the palace, whereupon the watchman gave her a clout and chased her away. She turned and came back and turned and came back again. The governor's daughter was watching, and having pity on the old woman, she called her father's attention to what was going on.

The governor called for the woman and, on hearing what she wanted, sent her son to learn a trade. The boy went to work for a blacksmith, but before an hour had passed, he had knocked the blacksmith's hand with the hammer instead of the anvil. The blacksmith threw him out, whereupon he went to work for a cobbler. But before two hours had passed, he had pushed the awl into the cobbler's hand, and he ran away.

The boy left the town and went on and on until he came to a magnificent palace. He entered it and found no one inside. So he began wandering around. When he reached the palace court-yard, he came across a flock of sheep and goats and a huge herd of cattle tended by a devil. The young man approached him and was welcomed and invited to remain in the palace.

The devil became fond of the young man and taught him his sorcery and magic arts. One day the devil was about to leave the palace for a short time, so he handed the keys to the young man, saying, "You may do what you please in the six rooms of this palace but do not dare enter the seventh room." So saying he went off.

Immediately the young man opened the seventh room, and lo! what did he see inside? Dead men suspended from ropes. Only one of them was still breathing. The young man freed him by cutting the rope, and the victim revealed that this was the deed of the devil. "First he teaches his pupils magic arts, and then he hangs them."

The young man ran away from the palace and back to the town. He knew well that the mighty devil would chase him, so he used his knowledge of sorcery to transform himself into a noble horse. He told his mother to sell him to the governor but on no account to part with the bit and the reins.

That very day the devil recognized him in the governor's

palace, so the young man ran away and by means of his magic art transformed himself into a beautiful house. The governor bought the house, but within six hours it had crumbled into dust. The young man changed himself into a worthy mule. But the devil succeeded in buying the mule, together with the bit and the reins, from the boy's mother.

The devil brought the mule to the seaside and tried to drown him, whereupon the mule turned into a fish and plunged into the sea. The devil jumped after him, so the fish changed into an eagle and soared into the heavens above. Again the devil pursued him, whereupon the eagle turned into a ring and fell under the armpit of the governor's daughter. What did she do? She caught hold of the ring and put it into her jewelry box. The devil went in search of the governor and persuaded him to bring forth the ring. However, the ring turned into a peach, and when they sent for it, they found a pomegranate in its place. The governor grasped the pomegranate in his hands, whereupon it fell on the ground scattering its seeds. Instantly the devil changed into a chicken and swallowed all the seeds except one, which changed into a knife and slaughtered the cock. Then the knife transformed itself into a handsome man.

The governor was simply overjoyed to give him his daughter in marriage.

· 56 ·   *The Three Brothers*

IFA 22. Recorded by Elisheva Schoenfeld from Mordechai "Marko" Litsi, born in Turkey.

Type 550, Search for the Golden Bird. This extremely popular tale is reported throughout Europe in numerous variants and from Turkey, India, Indonesia, and Africa. In America it is found in the French, Spanish, and Negro traditions. In connection with the gift of three hairs in Arabic folktales, see E. Littmann, Arabische Märchen, *s.v. "Haare," p. 446. The additional Motifs D786.1, "Disenchantment by song," and H12, "Recogni-*

tion by song," bear witness to the singing ability of the narrator.
The song is sung twice in the story.

   This tale type is well represented in IFA. Elements are known
in central Asia; three texts from Uzbekistan were published by
M. I. Shewerdin, Vol. I, Nos. 22, 29, 41, and one from the Uigu-
rian cultural area is given in M. N. Kabirov–V. F. Shahmatov,
No. 23. Four versions are known in the Caucasus; see A. H.
Bjazirov, Nos. 11, 15; S. Britajev-K. Kasbekov, No. 32; N. Kapieva, No. 1. A Sephardic–Jewish variant is given in M. Grunwald, No. 4.

• MANY YEARS AGO there lived a king with his three sons in a
magnificent palace surrounded by beautiful gardens. In one of
these gardens there was a tree that bore pure golden apples.
Every morning the king went to his garden to count his apples,
and every day one of them was missing, even though there were
many watchmen guarding the premises. The king ordered his
sons to keep watch under the golden apple tree in order to detect
the thief.

   The first to keep watch was the eldest son. In the evening he
sat by the tree and remained on guard for a long time. But at
midnight he fell asleep. When he woke up in the morning, one
apple was missing. And the same thing happened to the second
son; he also fell asleep.

   The king was angry with his two sons, and on the third night
he sent his youngest son to keep watch. He put a sword between
his legs so that when he became sleepy and his head fell on his
chest, the sword prodded him and woke him up. Thus he managed not to fall asleep at midnight. At three o'clock in the morning a beautiful big bird came and tried to steal an apple, but the
theft was prevented by the youngest son. In the morning he recounted this to the father.

   The king commanded his three sons to go out in search of the
thief and to find the stolen golden apples. The sons buckled their
swords and set off. At midday they reached a crossroads, branch-
ing in three directions. There they sat down and ate their meal. A
hungry dog approached and pleaded with his eyes for bread. The

older brothers chased the dog away being loath to feed him. Whereupon the youngest son beckoned to him and shared his food with the poor animal.

When they had eaten their fill, the brothers set off upon different paths. The eldest brother turned to the right, the second brother went straight ahead, and the youngest brother went to the left. The dog stayed close to the youngest brother who had been so good to him. After a short distance he suddenly began to speak, "If you go on in this direction you will run into a great danger. A little farther on there is a tap and nearby a mug. You will surely want to drink in this heat. Take the mug, and drink as much as you want, but on no account make a noise while replacing the mug."

The young man looked around in surprise to see who was talking to him. He did not believe that the dog could speak like a human being.

Said the dog, "It is I, the dog beside you, who is talking. I am going to leave you now. Take three hairs of mine. Burn one of them if you are in danger, and I will come to your aid." The young man took the hairs and put them into his pocket, whereupon the dog disappeared.

After a short time the young man reached the tap. He took the mug, and after drinking he tried to replace it without making a sound. However the glass made a muffled ring. Suddenly a tall, plump woman appeared. "What are you doing here?" she shouted. "Why have you come to disturb me?" The young man was abashed by the woman's appearance, but he explained his errand quietly. He told about his father, the king, the theft of the golden apples, and his search for the thief.

"You will need a special horse to find the thief," said the tall, plump woman, "and such a horse you will find only in the next town. But if you go there, you will never return."

The young man did not give two thoughts to the matter and set off. After he had gone a little distance, he came across the dog again. The young man told the dog of the woman's words, and the dog urged him, "There is a stable in the town; approach stealthily, open the door, and free the horse. Mount and gallop away as quickly as possible. Do not look backward, just forward.

Only in such a way will you be able to save yourself from death."
The dog finished speaking and disappeared.

The young man came to the town. He found the stable, opened
the door, and took out a horse. Swiftly he closed the door,
mounted the horse, and at full speed galloped away beyond the
outskirts of the town. He did not look behind, even though he
heard the people of the town shouting, "Come back! Come back!
Be our king!"

The young man returned to the tall, plump woman. How surprised she was to see him safe and sound. She told him that the
most dangerous deed still lay ahead—to catch the thief. "It is a
girl; she sits in a tree surrounded by marble statues. They were
once young men who desired her love, and she has turned them
into statues. Only if you win her love, will you not be turned into
a statue."

"I would like to ride there," said the young man. "I shall try
my luck. Maybe I shall succeed in catching the thief and return
the stolen apples to my father."

The young man mounted his horse and set out in search of the
tree surrounded by statues. Before evening he found a large site
strewn with marble statues. In the center there was a big tree
with wide branches stretching to the ground. Suddenly the horse
halted. The young man looked down and saw the horse's legs
had been turned into stone. Although he did not see anyone, he
turned to the tree and said, "Why are you so wicked? Why do
you turn living people into statues? No wonder that no man cares
for your love."

Suddenly he felt that half of his body had turned into
stone. He was terrified. Then he remembered what the tall,
plump woman had told him, and he began to sing a song of
love:

> "Come down fair maiden,
>   Come down from the tree,
>   Come down fair maiden,
>   Reveal yourself to me."

The young man looked at himself and his horse, and once again
they were flesh and blood. The beautiful girl-thief climbed down

the tree and went toward him, carrying the golden apples. The young man picked her up, mounted his horse, and set off.

When they came to the crossroads they met the other brothers. The youngest brother related how he had found the thief, and he showed them the golden apples. They envied him, and bitter was their envy. While one of them went ahead with the girl, the other one grabbed hold of the youngest brother, burned out his eyes with a red-hot iron, and threw him into a pit not far from the meeting place.

The youngest brother remembered the dog's three hairs. He pulled one from his pocket and burned it. Immediately the dog came to the opening of the pit and saw his master in great distress. Not far from the pit a man passed by. The dog rushed to him and asked the man to follow him. The man understood the dog, and approaching the pit, he saw the young man below. He pulled him out with a rope, whereupon the dog disappeared.

The young man had succeeded in getting out of the pit, but where should he go now? How could he find his way home when he could no longer see? He burned the second hair, and the dog appeared again and led him under a tree. "You will regain your eyesight, if you rub your eyes with the blood of a bird," he said and disappeared.

The young man became very sad. "How can I catch a bird when darkness enfolds me?" Suddenly he heard a bird above his head. "Do not leave the nest before you are ready to fly. There is a man below waiting to take the life of one of you; he wants to rub his eyes with your blood so as to regain his sight."

One of the wee birds was thinking to himself, "I would like to help this poor man." And it jumped from the nest onto the young man's forehead. He grasped the bird in his hands, kissed his beak, and rubbed his eyes with its blood; and lo! light came to his eyes.

The young man returned to his father's palace, but no one recognized him there. So he went to the city, dressed himself up as a merchant, and bought clothes to sell at his father's palace. When he arrived at the courtyard, he saw the young girl at the window above. He began to sing the song that he had sung when he stood by the tree surrounded by statues.

> "Come down, fair maiden,
> Come down from the tree,
> Come down, fair maiden,
> Reveal yourself to me."

The young girl heard the song, hurried to the young man, and kissed him. Then she went to the king and told him the truth. "This is your son who found me in his search for the golden apples."

The king listened to the story and embraced and kissed his faithful son. Then he ordered his guards to throw the two elder sons into prison for life.

· 57 · Who Is Blessed with the Realm, Riches, and Honor?

IFA 346. Recorded by S. Bashri from her eldest brother, Zakharia Bashri, about fifty years of age, born in a village near Sadda, southeastern Yemen.

This is a form of Type 923B, The Princess Who Was Responsible for Her Own Fortune. Cf. Jewish literary versions given in M. Gaster, The Exempla of the Rabbis, No. 148, and Gaster (ed.), Ma'aseh Book, No. 68; a Jewish oral text from eastern Europe can be found in Y. L. Cahan (1931), No. 13.

Type 923B is reported mainly from the Orient, especially India. In European countries it is popular in the form of Type 923, Love like Salt, the King Lear story. It is Grimm's tale No. 179, "The Goose Girl by the Spring." Additional motifs in the present text are B123.1, "Wise serpent," N452, "Secret remedy overheard in conversation of animals (witches)," B161.2, "Fortune learned from serpent," and B562.1, "Animal shows man treasure." The treasure-giving snake is very popular in Eastern folklore; see W. Eberhard-P. N. Boratav, Index, s.v. "Schlange," pp. 487–88. An Uzbek variant of Type 923B is given in M. I. Shewerdin, Vol. I, No. 31, and a Kurdish one in E. S. Druzhinina, No. 23.

• IN THE HEAT of midday, a handsome and comely prince noticed two snakes twisted round each other. Suddenly one of them crawled toward the prince and said to him in a human voice, "Save me from the hands of my enemy. I have no strength left in me."

The prince was astonished and said to the pleading snake, escaping from his pursuer, "Swear that you will do me no evil and that you will leave me immediately your enemy is out of sight."

"I swear," promised the snake, in an imploring voice.

Then the snake entered the prince's mouth and penetrated into his body. After the other snake had left in disappointment, the prince called to the snake whom he had delivered, "Now get out of my stomach." But his call was in vain. The snake refused to budge and said, "I will remain here all my life. I like this place and feel at home here."

From that time on the prince's flesh began to waste away, and his stomach became so swollen that he could not move his limbs. Little by little he became so very ugly that even his own father, the king, lost interest in him and left his son to his own fate. When the prince saw that he had become a burden in the palace, and no one was concerned about him, he left the town and began to roam from place to place, begging for alms.

One day he came to a place in which a sultan dwelt in a palace with his three beautiful daughters. In the morning the sultan would call out to his eldest daughter, "Who is blessed with the realm, riches, and honor, my daughter?"

"You, father," the eldest daughter would reply.

Then the sultan would call out to his second daughter and ask her, "Who is blessed with the realm, riches, and honor?" She would reply, "You, father."

Then he would ask his youngest daughter, "Who is blessed with the realm, riches, and honor?" and she would always reply, "The Lord alone, my father." Each time the youngest daughter was given violent blows, but she never took her words back.

From day to day the sultan's anger with his youngest daughter grew, until one day he swore, "Tomorrow I shall give my daughter to the first beggar who passes the palace."

Early the next morning, looking through the window, he saw an ugly beggar with a swollen stomach, dressed in torn clothes and lying prostrate by the palace walls. He called his youngest daughter and asked, "Who is blessed with the realm, riches, and honor, my daughter?"

"The Almighty alone, my father!" answered the daughter as usual.

Immediately he called the beggar and pointing to his daughter, commanded, "Take her for your wife!"

"Do not make a fool of me, my lord," implored the beggar in confusion, "I am in a difficult plight."

"I mean what I say!" exclaimed the sultan. "Take her and depart."

While the man stood in bewilderment, the princess took him by his hand and said, "You are my luck, and this is my fate." And together they left the palace.

They arrived at last at a field beyond the town. There the princess put up a hut, made a bed, and helped the sick man to lie down. Next day she went to the forest, chopped wood, piled it up, and made a log fire. What a wonderfully good smell, as fragrant as the Garden of Eden!

The princess realized that the wood was of a special kind, and its fragrance excelled the finest perfume. She chopped down more trees, and every day, in disguise, she went to the market of the nearby town to sell the logs. When the citizens discovered the amazing properties of the wood, they began to buy more and more of the logs, and the couple did not suffer from hunger.

One day the princess lay the sick man to rest on a stone in the shadow of a tree while she herself was chopping wood. Suddenly she heard a sound like the croaking of a frog. Looking at the sick man, now asleep, she realized that the croaking came from his stomach. Suddenly she heard another sound, the voice of a snake whispering from outside, "Are you not ashamed to croak from a man's stomach?"

The princess listened carefully because she wanted to hear the answer, and indeed, it came from the snake within the stomach. "I feel at home here and am living in comfort. But you are stupid and miserable, working all day long to find bread for your starving soul."

"Get out, you coward, shameful liar, who repays evil for good," angrily whispered the snake from outside.

The snake within answered, "You are no better than I am. I know your secret very well. Under the nearby stone your stolen treasure is hidden."

"I have enough besides this treasure," was the answer. "But you are a traitor. What have you done to the worthy prince who saved you from death? If the girl had been wise enough, she would have taken leaves from the tree above, ground them, brewed a drink, and routed you."

After he had finished speaking, the princess sighed with relief and gratitude. Immediately she plucked the leaves from the tree above, ground them, and brewed a drink. Then she handed it to the prince, who drank the draft without a word. Suddenly he felt a severe stomach-ache. The snake came out from his stomach, bit by bit.

All the time the prince suffered great pains, and at last he fainted. The girl tended him with care, and after several weeks the prince had regained his health and was hale and hearty. Then the girl dug under the stone, and lo! she found the snake's treasure underneath it. In the months that followed the couple set about planning their palace. Both of them showed great diligence and knowledge and soon the building was completed. It was indeed a beautiful palace and contained a special reception hall for beggars and passers-by.

When everything was ready, the couple moved in. One day, after many years had passed, two old men appeared amongst the beggars visiting the reception hall. The couple recognized them as their parents; it so happened that the two kings had become poor, and their heartless children had driven them away. Now they came, shabbily dressed, after having tramped from place to place with beggars they met on their way. The couple invited the two old men to change their clothes and to tell their life stories. When they had finished, the young couple revealed who they were. The fathers recognized their children and listened the night long to each other's adventures.

There was great rejoicing in the palace, and before morning the girl's father concluded, "You were right, my daughter. The realm, riches, and honor are the Almighty's alone."

·58· *The Ten Serpents*

IFA 386. Recorded by Abraham Shani from a washerwoman born in Bukhara.

Type 425, The Search for the Lost Husband. *All five episodes of this international tale are discernible: I, "The Monster as Husband"; II, "Disenchantment of the Monster"; III, "Loss of the Husband"; IV, "Search for Husband"; V, "Recovery of Husband." For Sephardic-Jewish versions, see J. Meyuhas,* Oriental Folktales *(Hebrew), No. 5, and M. Grunwald, Nos. 3, 6, 9, 47. A Jewish variant from eastern Europe is given in Y. L. Cahan (1938), No. 20.*

The most recent monograph is by J. O. Swahn, The Tale of Cupid and Psyche *(Lund, 1955), which has a full bibliography and distributional maps. A total of 580 texts has been collected in six countries alone: Sweden, Norway, Ireland, France, Germany, and Italy. Under Type 425A,* The Monster (Animal) as Bridegroom, *which is the Cupid and Psyche form, seventy-one Greek texts are cited. Recent Greek versions are in R. M. Dawkins,* Modern Greek Folktales, *No. 16. In North America the tale is common in French and Spanish traditions and among Negroes of the West Indies. The first literary treatment, dating from the second century* A.D., *is in Apuleius,* The Golden Ass.

The tale can now be seen to be popular in Asia and has been reported from India (S. Thompson and W. E. Roberts, Types of Indic Oral Tales, *p. 62), Turkey (W. Eberhard-P. N. Boratav, Nos. 93, 95, 96, 98, 99, 100–106), Palestinian Arabs (C. G. Campbell [1954], pp. 105–8), Iraq (F. S. Stevens, Nos. 6, 11), central Asia (M. I. Shewerdin, Vol. I, Nos. 42, 55, and Vol. II, Nos. 86, 139), and the Caucasus (A. H. Bjazirov, No. 8, and E. S. Druzhinina, No. 7).*

• ONCE UPON A TIME there was a poor orphan who was diligent and righteous. One night, in a dream, an old man appeared before him and put a diamond in his hand, saying, "With this diamond you will become rich, build a house, and wed. You will have but one daughter, whom you must guard carefully, because you will have to return her in exchange for the diamond. If you do not heed this warning, you will become poor once again." The old man finished his words and disappeared.

In the morning the boy awoke and found a huge diamond in his hand. He sold it, bought goods, and began to wander from town to town, carrying on trade.

Years passed, and the youth became a very rich merchant, the husband of a pretty wife, and the father of a beautiful daughter without match in all the kingdom.

One day, when the merchant was returning home, a serpent suddenly crept out of the forest. The merchant tried to make his escape, but it was as if his legs were stuck to the spot; he could not move. And the serpent crept nearer and nearer. Suddenly the merchant heard a voice from above, "Venerable sir! If you want to escape death, give me your daughter in marriage. If not, the serpent will bite you to death."

Remembering his dream and the warning of the old man, the merchant agreed, whereupon the snake vanished and the merchant found he could move once more. As he began walking away, he heard the mysterious voice again: "Venerable merchant, if you cheat me, you will die."

The merchant went home, and lo, his house, garden, and even his servants had disappeared. In their place stood a poor miserable hut. The merchant's wife and daughter were both poorly clad, and suddenly he noticed that his own clothes, too, were in tatters. Immediately he regretted what he had said to the mysterious voice, and he related to his family all that had happened to him. His sorrow was so great that he wished to die.

When his beautiful and obedient daughter saw her father's distress, she said, "I will fulfil your promise, father. I am willing to live a life of anguish so that you may be spared."

Weeks passed, months went by, and the merchant's family became used to their poverty. Then one night there was a knock at the door of the hut, and on opening it, the merchant beheld a huge and terrible serpent. It opened its mouth and said in a human voice, "I am the stranger to whom you promised your daughter."

The father turned to his daughter in anguish and said, "I prefer to die than to give you up in marriage to this terrible monster."

However, the obedient daughter sacrificed herself to marry the serpent in order to save her father's life. The snake gave her a ring as a token of betrothal, and they went to the second room and shut the door. Suddenly the serpent shook himself and shed his skin, and lo! a handsome youth stood in front of the daughter. He said to her: "If you want to live happily with me, do not ask any questions and do not tell anyone, even your parents, what you have seen. Every morning I will leave you, but I will return at nightfall."

You can well imagine that the daughter fell in love with this handsome young man at first sight and promised to carry out his bidding.

In the morning the daughter awoke to find that the serpent was no longer there. In the meantime her parents, who had not slept a wink the whole night, were full of fear and anxiety for their daughter. They did not believe their eyes when they saw her leaving the room, safe and sound, in fact, joyous and happy. They began to shower her with questions, but their daughter, who had always respected them, refused to answer.

A few nights passed, and the parents began to rebuke their daughter for hiding the truth from them who loved her so dearly. At last the daughter broke down and disclosed the secret. That evening the serpent appeared but did not shed his skin as usual. He said in a sad voice, "As you have broken your promise, I shall have to leave you. Do not search for me anywhere because you will not find me."

The daughter did not even have time to apologize; in the winking of an eye, the serpent had vanished. The daughter became very sad. She would lock herself everyday in her room, refusing to admit anyone.

Nearby lived a poor family. It so happened that one day their daughter was playing in the street with her doll. A dog passed by, seized the doll, and scampered off. The child followed him. The dog went beyond the town, and the child still trailed behind him. There was always the same distance between them.

Suddenly a fox jumped out of the bushes and chased the dog. The dog became frightened, dropped the doll, and ran away. When the child reached the spot, she found the opening of a burrow, but the doll was not there. The child realized that the doll had fallen down the burrow, and she began to crawl inside. Neither the darkness around nor her many scratches made her despondent, and she crawled on until she reached a wide opening. She climbed through the opening, and there, before her eyes, was a magnificent palace surrounded by a lovely garden. And just near the opening of the burrow lay her doll. The child had not eaten anything all day, and she felt very hungry, so she entered the palace in search of food. She found there two large rooms; in the first one there was a table laden with ten dishes of food, and in the second one ten beds made up for the night. When the child approached the table, she heard voices from outside, so she hid herself under one of the beds. Suddenly into the room crawled ten huge serpents, terrible to behold.

The terrified child was on the point of screaming when the serpents shook themselves and shed their skins. They were no longer serpents but ten handsome young men, and they threw their skins out of the window. Then they knelt down and prayed, a prayer no less strange than anything the child had already seen. And these were the words of the prayer:

"We pray for a fair maiden to come hither, burn our skins, and rescue us."

After praying, the young men ate their fill and then went to bed. As the child hid under one of the beds, she saw the man sleeping above her take out a handkerchief from his pocket and kiss it. The child immediately recognized whose handkerchief it was. She was very tired and fell asleep. In the morning, when she awoke, the serpents had vanished. So the girl left the palace and set off for the town, looking carefully in all directions so as to remember the way. She decided to go straight to the merchant's daughter and to tell her of the handkerchief and all that she had seen; so she did. Immediately both of them ran together to the underground palace and hid themselves under one of the beds.

Everything happened as on the previous evening. When the serpents changed into men, the merchant's daughter recognized her beloved husband immediately. She waited patiently till nightfall, and when the young men were asleep, she went outside and burned their skins.

Morning came and the youths arose and saw what had happened. How they danced for joy! The merchant's daughter embraced her husband, and this is the story he told her: "We were ten princes. Our mother died, and our father remarried and had another son. Our stepmother bewitched all of us to ensure that her own son would succeed to the throne. Now that our skins have been burned, the witch has also been burned, and her spell is broken."

That same night the merchant dreamed of the same old man who had given him the diamond in a dream. The old man now freed him from his vow.

A wonderful wedding was arranged that same day, and people came from near and from far. When the old king died, the young couple succeeded to the throne, and they were beloved by all because they lived modestly, gave charity freely, and dealt out justice all the days of their life.

Part VIII
Wise Men

·59· The Lion Who Walked in the Garden

IFA 37. Recorded by Elisheva Schoenfeld in Affula in 1956 from Obadia Pervi of Yemen.

Type 891B*, The King's Glove. This story recurs frequently in the Arabic folk traditions assembled by René Basset, in Mille et un contes, récits et légendes Arabes *(3 vols.), and V. Chauvin, in* Bibliographie des ouvrages arabes *(12 vols.). See also* Thousand and One Nights, *trans. E. Littmann, III, 539. But here it has a strong Jewish flavor: the Bible reforms the king. The parable may be of Jewish origin, as the metaphor "a woman—a garden," based on a biblical verse ("A garden inclosed is my sister, my spouse," Song of Songs 4: 12) is common in the ancient Agadic literature. See Jacob Nacht,* Symbols of Women *(Tel Aviv, 1959), p. 76 ff. (Hebrew). Also common are the Motifs T320.4, "Wife escapes lust of king by shaming him," K2110.1, "Calumniated wife," T323, "Escaped from undesired lover by strategy," and N455.6, "Husband learns of wife's fidelity," through H580, "An enigmatic statement."*

Jewish literary versions are given in M. J. Bin Gorion, Der Born Judas, *I, 254–62.*

• ONCE THERE was a king who was very fond of women, and no young and attractive girl was ever safe from his grasp. Not far from the king's palace there lived a Jewish *haham* (sage) who had a beautiful wife. He knew the king's passion and used to bolt the door of his house every day before leaving for the yeshiva (house of learning).

One day he forgot to bolt the door, an opportunity for which the king had been waiting for a long, long time. Thus the king entered the house of the sage and requested his wife to submit to him. In dismay, she begged the king to wait a while until she had dressed and beautified herself in his honor. The king agreed to her plea, whereupon she gave him the Book of Torah to read until she had finished her toilet. Of course she did not change her garments but ran to her neighbors and hid there.

Meanwhile the king read the Book of the Torah. He read for an hour, two hours, three hours. The woman did not return, and by then it was lunch time. The king got up from his seat and put a bag of gold coins on the wife's bed together with his rosary. Then he took with him the Book of the Torah and went away because he was anxious to avoid her husband.

When the clever woman learned from her neighbor that the king had left her house, she came back and went straight to the kitchen to prepare lunch for herself and her husband. After half an hour her husband returned, and they entered the bedroom together. The haham found the bag of coins and the king's rosary on his wife's bed. He looked at them and gazed at his wife. "The king was here with you!" he muttered under his breath. His wife remained silent. She thought, "Whatever I say, my husband will not believe me." From that day the sage neither came to his wife nor talked to her.

The wife became very ill, and there was not a doctor who could cure her. When her end seemed near, her three brothers, who lived in another town, were called. When they arrived, the woman told them of the king's visit to her house and how she had hidden in the house of her neighbors. She also told them that her husband no longer trusted her and would not even speak to her.

The brothers immediately asked their brother-in-law to go with them to the king. He agreed, and they went to the king and stood before him and his ministers.

"Your majesty, the king," one of the brothers began his story, "some years ago, our father died, blessed be his memory. He bequeathed us a house, a vineyard, fields, and a garden. We are three brothers, so one of us took the house, one of us the vineyards, and one of us the fields. We did not, however, know what to do with the garden. Then along came this man" (here the storyteller pointed to the haham) "and offered to cultivate it. We agreed and signed a contract. Therein it is written that he should be allowed to benefit from the garden, but on one condition: that he tend to it. Lately this man has not abided by the contract. He has not tilled the land, he has not cleared out the thorns and weeds, he has not dug the ground. And the garden has become neglected. We are requesting, therefore, that he give us back our garden."

"What have you to say?" said the king to the wise man.

"Indeed," said the haham, "these men are right in accusing me of neglecting the garden. But not always was I neglectful. I cultivated it faithfully until I saw therein the footsteps of the king's lion, who took away the fruit. I am also afraid that he may come back and take even my life."

The king understood the riddle-language, and it pleased him very much. He answered the wise man thus: "It is known to me that my lion wanders in the town. But he will not do so any more because I shall surround his den with high thick walls. Moreover, even while prowling in your garden, he did not take any fruit or any flowers therein. The walls were too high, and he could not climb over them. He cut off but one bunch of grapes, and I shall return it to you." The king took out the Book of the Torah from his coat and handed it to the haham.

The wise man understood the king's words. He returned home and began once more to talk to his wife and to pay attention to her. Before long she recovered from her illness, and both of them lived thereafter in happiness and contentment.

·60· *A Servant When He Reigns*

IFA 280. Recorded by Zvi Moshe Haimovitch from Josef Shmuli, over seventy years old. The storyteller, born in Basra, Iraq, is now a resident of the Malben Home for the Aged in Pardes Hannah.

The well-known Motifs H171.2, "Bird indicates election of emperor," L113.1.7, "Slave as hero," L165, "Lowly boy becomes king," and J913, "King has earthen vessels placed on table among the golden ones," are used here within a framework of a didactic parable (mashal) on spurning false pride, whose moral (nimshal) the storyteller no longer remembered. The meaning of the biblical quotation (Prov. 30:22) which gives the title to the story is completely different here from that in the original context. The humility of the king may be intended as an allusion to man's lowliness as reflected in such phrases as the "fetid drop" and the "place of dust, worms, and maggots" in the "Teaching of Our Fathers" (Philip Blackman (ed.), Mishnayot, Vol. IV [London, 1954], chap. iii, p. 505).

• IN A CERTAIN kingdom in olden days it was the custom to choose a king by the will of heaven. A rare bird, known as the Bird of Happiness, was sent forth when the king died, and whomever's head the bird rested on, he became king. Once it came to pass that when the ruling king died and the bird was sent forth, it rested on a slave's head. The slave used to earn his daily bread playing the drum and dancing at weddings, dressed up in a feathered cap and wearing a belt made of lamb's hooves.

When the slave was chosen as king, he ordered a small hut built near the royal palace. He put inside it his treasured possessions—his feathered cap, his belt made of lamb's hooves, and his drum, as well as a big mirror.

The ministers wondered very much and asked the king to explain his strange behavior. "You have to guard your dignity even when you are alone," they reprimanded him.

The king answered, "I was a slave before I became king. Thus I want to remind myself that I was a slave. Only then will I not imagine myself greater than you and other men; only then will I not feel proud in my heart."

• 61 •   *What Melody Is the Sweetest?*

IFA 1182. Narrated by Zvulun Kort from Afghanistan, now resident in Tel Aviv.

For other answers to the riddle of the superlative, "What is the sweetest sound?" (bell-ringing, God's word, and so on), see Motif H635, "Riddle: What is the sweetest sound?" The riddle is sometimes part of Type 875, The Clever Peasant Girl, or 922, The Shepherd Substituting for the Priest Answers the King's Questions, both world-wide tales. For other riddles of superlatives, see No. 68 (in this book), "Two Madmen" (IFA 309).

• SHAH ABBAS of Persia was a man of wit who liked to converse in parables. Among his ministers was Merza Azki, who understood his parables well.

One day the Shah was holding court with his ministers, discussing the ways of this world. Thereon he asked his ministers: "What is the sweetest melody?"

One answered, "The melody of the flute."

"No," answered another minister. "The melody of the harp is the most pleasant to the ear."

The third remarked, "Neither one nor the other! The violin has the finest tone."

Thus a bitter dispute arose.

Merza Zaki was silent and did not say anything. Days passed. Then Merza Zaki invited the Shah and the rulers of the state to a banquet arranged in their honor. Musicians entertained the honored guests on all kinds of instruments. But how strange, the table bore no refreshments. The guests were without food and drink. You must know that in the East the tables are always laden with delicacies at a banquet, and when the guests have eaten and drunk their fill, there is still more food, and copper vessels of meat and rice are brought to the loaded tables. Now where was the food? It was embarrassing to ask, so the guests just went on sitting till midnight. Then Merza Zaki beckoned to the head waiter, and he brought a vessel of cooked food into the room and beat the lid of the pot with a big spoon. Clink! Clink!

All the guests breathed a sigh of relief. Indeed it was time. Then Shah Abbas said, "The clink of dishes in the ears of a hungry man—this is the sweetest melody."

•62• The Tailor's and the Lord's Work

IFA 639. Recorded by N. Schwarzstein in Jerusalem from I. Stil, born in Hungary.

For another version, see A. Druyanov, Vol. I, No. 125. This jest contains Motif J1115.4, "Clever tailor."

• A RABBI ordered a pair of trousers. His tailor promised: "I shall bring them to you within a week, next Friday."

The tailor, however, did not keep his promise and brought the trousers three days late.

The rabbi tried on the trousers and was well satisfied because they fit him perfectly. He paid the tailor and asked, "Explain to me why the Lord took six days only to create the world and to make one pair of trousers you took ten days."

The tailor lifted his head and answered seriously, "My Rabbi! Look at *my* work. There is not a defect therein. Now look at the world, the work of the Almighty, blessed be he."

.63. *This Too Will Pass*

IFA 126. Recorded by Heda Jason, a Hebrew University student, from D. Franko, a merchant, born in Turkey.

In the journal of the Israel Folklore Society, Yeda-ʿAm, No. 9 (February, 1952), p. 14, Rabbi Y. L. Avida (formerly Zlotnik) and Dr. Yom-Tov Lewinski offer several patterns and explanations of the Hebrew magic formula "GZY" as being an abbreviation of the Hebrew "Gamzu yaʿavor" (This Too Shall Pass). They quote several printed versions of the story. During World War II a company in the United States sold "GZY" good luck rings "For Our Boys in the Service" with the three Hebrew letters engraved on the ring. Motifs H86.3, "Ring with names inscribed on it," D1317.5, "Magic ring gives warning," and D1500.1.8, "Magic amulet cures disease," are present.

• KING SOLOMON once searched for a cure against depression. He assembled his wise men together. They meditated for a long time and then gave him the following advice: Make yourself a ring and have thereon engraved the words "This too will pass."

The King carried out the advice. He had the ring made and wore it constantly. Every time he felt sad and depressed, he looked at the ring, whereon his mood would change and he would feel cheerful.

·64· The Rambam and the Bottle of Poison

IFA 666. Recorded by Sami Saati, a young laborer, as heard from his parents in Iraq.

This tale contains Motifs N646, "Man thinks to end life by drinking poisonous water, but it cures him," D1500.1.16, "Magic healing bottle," J1115.2, "Clever physician," and F956, "Extraordinary diagnosis." Maimonides (1135–1204) wrote a special treatise in 1199 "On Poisons and the Protection against Deadly Remedies"; a discussion of "The Medical Works of Maimonides," by M. Meyerhof, is included in Essays on Maimonides, ed. S. W. Baron (New York, 1941), pp. 265–300. Compare the present tale with the biblical account of how Moses cured the people of Israel from serpent bites with a copper image of a snake (Num. 21:6–9). For references to postbiblical literature, see L. Ginzberg, The Legends of the Jews, III, 336, and VI, 115–16.

For Maimonides in Jewish folktales and legends, see Jeshaja Berger, "Rambam in Folk-Legend," Massad, II (Tel Aviv, 1936), 216–38. "Rambam" is formed from the initial letters of the full name: Rabenu Moshe Ben Maimon.

• THE RAMBAM (Maimonides) was a famous doctor in his time. He also owned a pharmacy in which there were rows of medicine bottles. When a sick man came for treatment, the Rambam used to look at the medicine bottles, whereupon one of them would begin to shake. That very bottle was the remedy for the patient. Immediately the Rambam would climb up the ladder and bring down the medicine.

A patient once visited all the other doctors in the town, but they were unable to find a remedy for him. Then he came to the Rambam and told him of his troubles. The Rambam looked at the bottles, and behold! the bottle of poison began to shake. Then he said to the patient, "I am sorry. I have no remedy for you."

And to himself he pondered, "If anything was to happen to this patient on account of the poison, would not the blame be put on me?"

The patient went away in anger, walking on and on until he came to a forest. There he lay down to rest under the shade of a tree. His throat was parched with thirst, and he looked around for water. Suddenly he heard a dripping sound and saw drops of liquid trickling into a jar. He decided to get up and drink the water. He gulped it and immediately felt better. His sickness was over.

He returned to the Rambam and told him triumphantly what had happened. The Rambam said, "Go, please, to the same place and find out where the water is falling from."

The man returned to the forest and saw on one of the branches of the tree a huge snake that was dripping liquid from its mouth into the jar. The man returned to the Rambam and told him what he had seen.

The Rambam laughed and said, "The bottle of poison that began to shake at my pharmacy was the only remedy for you. I knew it, but I feared that the blame would be put on me if any disaster befell you."

Part IX
Numskulls

·65· The Passover Miracle

IFA 1855. Recorded by Miriam Sheli from her Tunisian-born father, Nahorai Sheli.

Type 1529, Thief Claims To Have Been Transformed into a Horse. *Another Jewish version of this type can be found in A. Druyanov, Vol. II, No. 1346, and a Jewish text from eastern Europe is recorded in Gross, pp. 408–9. For additional references, see R. Köhler-J. Bolte, I, 507–9. Turkish texts are noted in W. Eberhard-P. N. Boratav, No. 341 (III), "Die Diebe und der Bauer." The tale is known in the ancient Arabic literature (V. Chauvin, VII, 136; and R. Basset, I, 492). In the Spanish tradition it has been carried to Chile and the Philippines. Although no examples have yet been printed from the United States, R. M. Dorson has recorded a Polish text from Hipolith Gluski in Detroit, Michigan.*

• THE FEAST OF Passover was close at hand, and a poor Jew of the village had not even a single coin for his Seder meal. Thus he came to a rich Jew of the same village with a proposal. "Instead of giving me a hundred lira, why not let me take your donkey on loan?"

The rich Jew agreed of course. He would receive his donkey back without any loss of money.

On the market day preceding Passover the Jew brought the donkey for sale. The price was low enough, and the donkey was sold to a Bedawi. The Jew followed the Bedawi and his donkey on their way home. At night he entered the Bedawi's courtyard, stole the donkey, and brought it back to the rich Jew. Then he returned to the Bedawi's courtyard, hitched himself instead of the donkey, and waited.

In the morning the Bedawi found a man instead of a donkey. His heart was filled with fear. Immediately the donkey (the poor Jew) started to explain that he was in reality a man whom the demons had punished by transforming him into a donkey.

The Bedawi was shocked. He freed the man and asked him to

go and not to return. He exclaimed, "I do not want any ties with demons and with transformed men."

Now the Jew used the money from the sale of the donkey for the Passover meal.

On the next market day the rich Jew brought his donkey for sale. The Bedawi, who still had no donkey, came again to the market place in order to look for one. When he saw the donkey that he had bought a short time before, he approached him and whispered into his ears, "This time let somebody buy you who does not know you. You already made fun of me once. That is quite enough."

•66• *The One-Eyed Cadi*

IFA 1875. Recorded by Josef Shaar, an elementary-school teacher, from Suliman Shamen, born in San'a, the old capital of Yemen.

Type 1675, The Ox (Ass) as Mayor, and Motif J1882.2, "The ass as a mayor." This is primarily a literary anecdote, appearing in Eastern collections such as the A Thousand and One Nights *and among the jests of Hodscha Nasreddin (S. Thompson, The Folktale, p. 191). For bibliographical references, see V. Chauvin, VII, 170; A. Wesselski, Der Hodscha Nasreddin, Vol. I, p. 224, No. 63; and J. Bolte-G. Polívka, I, 59, n. 1. Type 1675 is reported from oral circulation chiefly in northern and eastern Europe, in India, and in the French tradition in Canada.*

A central Asian text, from Kazakhstan, appears in W. Sidel-nikov, No. 26; an Arab one is given in C. G. Campbell (1952), No. 30; and east European-Jewish ones can be found in N. Gross, pp. 110, 209–10.

• THE MOSLEM ministers in Yemen were from the "haughty" sect. They affirmed that when a Jewish father died the Jewishness of his sons was extinguished and that Moslems were commanded to convert these orphans, who had now become pure, to Islam. Imam Yodye, the king of Yemen, was a merciful king and was not strict in carrying out this religious precept in the city of San'a.

But the ministers, headed by the sons of the Alusa family, were unyielding in this matter. In every district where their weight was felt, they used to hunt out Jewish orphans, catch hold of them, and convert them to Islam by force.

A Jewish quarter in the city of San'a, Koa El Yehud, was a refuge for all orphans smuggled by their relatives from the towns and villages of Yemen. From time to time the men of Alusa used to pass by this Jewish quarter, and search for the smuggled orphans. The followers of Alusa were mostly empty and reckless men about whom Kohelet said, "There is no superiority of a man over an animal."

"Certainly there are orphans among them," said one of the men of Alusa when he entered the cheder and saw the teacher teaching his pupils the Torah. The teacher, who saw before him a *kabile*, said, "What! Do not you see that these are not children? Once they were young asses, and through much studying they have been transformed into children."

One of the children who understood the words of his teacher began to bray, and all the other children joined him.

"You see," said the teacher to the kabile. "When they stop learning, they turn into young asses again."

The cheder became a babel. The pupils' brays did not stop, and the kabile was convinced that the teacher spoke the truth.

"I have at home a young one-eyed ass," said the kabile. "Tomorrow I shall bring him to you, and I hope it won't be difficult for you to teach him and turn him into a boy."

The teacher was surprised at this request and said, "You will have to wait a long time."

"How long?"

"Three years."

"I am ready to wait, if only you can turn the ass into a boy. For many years now my wife and I have longed for a son, but the Almighty has not granted our wish."

When the kabile left the cheder and returned to his village, Beir El Asab, the teacher said to his pupils, "Our scholars, may they be blessed, permitted deception to unbelievers, informers, and collectors if it were a question of the safety of life."

On the following morning the kabile brought a one-eyed ass

to the cheder and said to the teacher, "I have brought the young ass to be taught. In three years I shall come to fetch him."

"I must tell you," the teacher warned the kabile, "that nobody should hear about this, and you must never come here on a visit, till you come here in three years time to take him back."

The teacher handed the ass to a kabile in another village and hoped that the whole incident would be forgotten and the hounding of Jewish orphans would no longer disturb the Jews.

The Kabile returned to Beir El Asab happy and joyous in his heart. He was sure that his ass would progress in the Jewish quarter and within three years would be turned into an intelligent being.

After three years the Kabile came back to the teacher and asked about the ass, which should by now have become a youth.

"Where is my boy? Where is my boy?" asked the kabile, and he began to search for him among the pupils. The teacher was surprised at first at this strange request, but then he remembered his promise. "He who intends to lie has to cast aside his evidence," thought the teacher in his heart, and he said to the kabile, "Your ass excelled as a pupil. He learned quickly, and this year he was appointed *cadi* (judge) in Demar."

"In Demar?" asked the kabile.

"Yes, in Demar," answered the teacher with assurance, knowing that the cadi of Demar was one-eyed.

The Kabile received the teacher's tidings with joy and went to Demar to look for the ass who had become a cadi. When he arrived in Demar, he saw that indeed the cadi was one-eyed.

"Do you not recognize me?" the kabile asked. "You are my one-eyed ass."

When the cadi of Demar, a respectable man and quick to anger, heard this blasphemy from the kabile, he took it as that of a madman and gave immediate orders for his arrest.

"Is this my reward?" called out the kabile. "I gave him my best hay, and now he treats me as a stranger."

All the explanations of the kabile did not help. His shouting and crying stirred up the cadi's anger even more, and he gave orders to chastise the kabile and to drive away the evil spirits from him.

·67· The Tailor with His Luck Locked Up

IFA 8. Recorded by Elisheva Schoenfeld from Mordechai "Marko" Litsi, born in Adrianople, Turkey.

The storyteller, though narrating in Hebrew, used Turkish expressions such as "tik-tik-tikandi," meaning "the luck is locked up." This story belongs to Type 947A, Bad Luck Cannot Be Arrested, which has been reported only in the east Mediterranean area. See W. Eberhard-P. N. Boratav, No. 131, "Der Unglücksmann" (III), for Turkish examples. However, a similar story from central Asia appears in M. I. Shewerdin, Vol. 1, No. 47, p. 348 (second tale). For another version, see No. 34 (in this book).

• THERE ONCE lived a tailor who sat from morning till night at his table stitching garments. He was a diligent and hard-working man, yet he did not grow rich.

"My luck is locked up, my luck is locked up," he used to say all day long.

One day the sultan and his vizier passed by the tailor's shop disguised in civilian clothes. When they heard the words of the tailor, they approached him, asking for suits to be made for them. The tailor agreed, and after a short time the suits were ready. The vizier came to fetch them, and he brought the tailor a roast chicken on a tray. However, he did not reveal that he had filled the chicken's stomach with gold coins. The tailor did not pay attention to the roast chicken. He just thanked the vizier and said that he would eat it when he grew hungry. Then he continued to stitch and to murmur, "My luck is locked up! My luck is locked up!"

The delicious smell that arose from the roast chicken attracted the attention of his neighbor, a rich merchant.

"Why do you not eat the chicken?" asked the merchant.

"I am not hungry. My luck is locked up, my luck is locked

up," answered the tailor. "Take the chicken, if you like. Just return the tray to me later on."

The merchant took the chicken home with him and, of course, found the coins inside. He hid them in his cupboard and returned the tray to the tailor without saying a single word about his find.

The next day the vizier came to fetch the tray. "Was the chicken tasty?" he asked.

"I did not eat it, as I was not hungry," answered the tailor. And he began to murmur, "My luck is locked up. My luck is locked up."

The vizier went away and pondered to himself how to help the tailor. He prepared a roast turkey, filled its stomach with gold, and brought it to the tailor.

Once more the tailor did not give a thought to the food, and once more the same neighbor who had taken the coins and hidden them in his cupboard took the turkey. He again enjoyed the meal and hid the coins he found inside. And the tailor continued to murmur, "My luck is locked up. My luck is locked up."

The neighbor returned the tray to the tailor, and the following day the vizier came to fetch it. "How are you? Did you enjoy the turkey?" he asked. "I did not eat it, as I was not hungry," answered the tailor. And he continued to murmur, "My luck is locked up, my luck is locked up."

"Indeed, your luck is locked up," said the vizier within his heart. Again he went to the palace, prepared a roast goose, filled it with gold coins, and brought it to the tailor. But this time again not the tailor but his rich neighbor enjoyed the food and acquired the coins hidden inside.

The same evening the vizier came to fetch the tray. When the tailor saw him coming, he said, "I see that you have once again brought me good food. Till now my rich neighbor enjoyed all your gifts, but today I am ready for a roast goose."

The vizier became very angry. "Your luck was in your own hands," he said. "There were gold coins inside the chicken, inside the turkey, and inside the goose. It is useless to help you. Your luck will always be locked up all the days of your life."

The tailor continued to stitch, murmuring, "My luck is locked up. My luck is locked up."

·68· Two Madmen

IFA 309. Recorded by Zvi Moshe Haimovitch from Menashe
Mashlad, born in Iraq and now a resident of the Malben Home
for the Aged in Neve Haim.

An unusual combination of a joke and a riddle. For another
version of the joke, see A. Druyanov, Vol. II, No. 1168. The same
three questions in the older Jewish literature can be found in
M. Gaster, The Exempla of the Rabbis, No. 434. For the questions, see Motifs H633.3, "What is sweetest: mother's breast,"
H645, "Riddle: what is the heaviest?" and H659.14, "Riddle:
what is easiest?" The humorous motifs are K1771, "Bluffing
threat," and J1116.1, "Clever madman."

• Two MADMEN were in a mental home in Baghdad. One of them,
named Nathan, had been well-to-do, but after losing all his
money he had had a breakdown. The other one, named Izhar,
was an educated man. He had fallen in love but was rejected,
whereupon he suffered deeply, and he too became ill.

Once when the doctor examined Nathan the patient complained
that evil men connected with him in business had testified that
he was mad and had him put in a mental home. He asked the
doctor to help him to get out of the home. The doctor, however,
gave him an evasive answer.

At the next examination, Nathan again pleaded with the doctor,
who promised he would try to help him. But the patient saw
that he was clutching at a straw. He had borne enough of this
treatment, and he decided to take the matter into his own hands.
And what did he do?

When night came, he climbed onto a wall of the mental home
and, with a stick in his hand, began knocking the wall and shouting the way one shouts when riding home in a hurry on a donkey.

The attendants at the mental home feared that the patient
would fall down and be killed and that they would be accused of
insufficient care. So they begged him to come down, making all
kinds of promises to him; but Nathan would not listen. Then the

matron came, carrying a new suit, and called to him, "Come put on your new suit before going home."

Nathan paid no attention to her words, and the onlookers were going out of their wits. Then came Izhar, his friend, who said to the doctor, "If you promise to set me free, I will get this man down from the wall."

The doctor agreed, whereupon Izhar asked for a big pair of scissors, and on being given them, he began to cut at the wall. While cutting he shouted, "You are falling down with the stones of the wall."

On hearing this, Nathan shouted, "Just a minute, I am coming down."

He was immediately caught and put into an isolation cell.

After this, Izhar asked the doctor to keep his promise and let him free.

"Wait a few days and I will keep my promise," replied the doctor.

"I am not going to wait any longer," answered Izhar, and he went to the director of the mental home and complained that the doctor had not kept his promise.

The director said, "I shall ask you three riddles, and if you are able to solve them, I shall let you go free."

Izhar agreed, whereupon the director asked, "What is sweeter than sweet? What is lighter than light? What is heavier than heavy?"

Izhar answered in the same order: "Milk the infant suckles from his mother's breast is sweeter than sweet. The embryo in the mother's womb is lighter than light. A cruel heart is heavier than heavy."

The director was satisfied with the patient's intelligence and granted him freedom.

·69· *The Two Husbands*

IFA 1749. Recorded by Abraham Ben Yaaḳov, an elementary-school principal, from an eighty-year-old woman born in Iraq.

This text combines Types 1284, Person Does Not Know Himself, *and 1406,* The Merry Wives Wager. *Motifs J2301, "Gullible husbands," and J2012.4, "Fool in new clothes does not know himself," are present. For another Jewish version employing the last motif, see A. Druyanov, Vol. II. No. 1139. A. Wesselski includes Asian versions of both types in his* Hodscha Nasreddin, *Vol. I, No. 298. For Turkish examples of Type 1406, see W. Eberhard-P. N. Boratav, No. 271, "Wer kann seinen Mann am besten betrügen?" Cf. an Arab text given by E. Littmann in* Arabische Märchen, *pp. 370–76. Type 1284 is reported from Belgium, Hungary, and India, whereas Type 1406 has a wider circulation throughout Europe. Recent recordings of Type 1406 from Kurdistan are in E. S. Druzhinina. Nos. 21, 39.*

Type 1284 appears independently in the next tale, No. 70 (IFA 1181).

• In an Eastern town lived a clever woman named Shafika. She had a stupid husband, and his name was Hangal. Shafika was a good housewife and she ran her home with knowledge and skill. She bore her fate in silence and with her own deeds covered up her husband's stupidity, without disclosing his shame in public.

One day a neighbor named Rahama visited her, and the two of them discussed the role of the man in the family. Rahama talked about courage and cleverness and the wealth of men. At this moment Shafika recalled her stupid husband, and she burst out in silent tears over her fate. Crying she spoke bitterly of the matchmakers who had not found her a good man as a husband. Then she decided to tell her neighbor all her troubles. As it is written: "A worry in the heart of a man has to be talked about."

"Oh! my dear neighbor," began Shafika, with a heartbreaking sigh. "What shall I say and what shall I recount? The Almighty has cursed me with a heavy curse and given me a husband who has in him all the stupidity of the entire world. He has caused me many misfortunes, and he doesn't know how to earn even a single pruta, all because of his exaggerated simpleness and because he does not know how to get on with people."

"The entire burden of the family rests on my shoulders and I am forced to work and to sweat out the day so as to earn some *pruta* for our very existence. And when the night comes, I have to arrange all the household needs. Woe is me! Woe is my fate! If you don't believe me, I shall call him here and show you an example of his stupidity."

At once Shafika called her husband and said, "Hangal, my husband, go to the roof and bring down a loaf of bread so you will have something to eat for lunch."

"As you wish, my wife," answered Hangal. "I am going immediately." Hangal went to the ladder and climbed up. When he was halfway up, he began to shout, "Shafika, Shafika! I am standing halfway up the ladder, and I don't know if I have to climb up or come down."

"Alas! Alas! stupid one!" answered Shafika. "If you have nothing in your hands, it means that you have not yet taken the loaf of bread and you must climb up. If you have a loaf of bread in your hands, it means that you have already been up and now you must climb down."

Hangal looked at his hands but did not find anything in them. Following his wife's advice, he climbed up to the roof, took the bread, and came down. When he was halfway down the ladder he stopped and shouted, "Shafika, Shafika! Again I'm in the middle of the ladder, and I don't know whether to climb up or to come down."

Again Shafika gave him the same advice. Hangal looked at his hands, found the bread, and came down.

"Did you see, my neighbor, my husband's stupidity?" asked Shafika and added, "That is my luck. I weep about it day and night, and there is no help."

Her neighbor consoled her and said, "My dear Shafika, do not become sad and do not let your husband's deeds seem so bad in your eyes. Those who make proverbs have said, 'Man is as black as coal, but he is also merciful.' It is better to have a husband like that than no husband at all. You know that a woman who has not a husband is not able to dress well, and she is forbidden to talk to other people. And now come close to me and I shall reveal a great secret to you. If you only knew the stupidity and foolishness of my husband, Shimon, you would be satisfied with what you have. You would lift up your eyes to the heavens and give thanks to the Almighty that he gave you a husband like Hangal.

My husband is worse than yours. If you don't believe me, come to my home and I shall show you an example of his stupidity."

So they went together to Rahama's house. Rahama took a jug, filled it with water, and then called her husband and said, "Here is a jug full of grain. Take it to the miller and ask him to grind it immediately because my neighbor will not leave until you return."

Shimon took the jug of water and went to the miller, saying to him, "My wife sends her greetings and says that we have a guest at home, so please will you grind the grain in this jug immediately so that I won't be late returning home."

When the miller saw the water in the jug and heard the way Shimon was speaking, he knew this was a stupid man in front of him. He decided thereupon to make a joke and have some fun on his account.

In a corner of the miller's house a Hindu was sleeping, and the miller said to Shimon, "Go and sleep next to the Hindu. When I have finished grinding the wheat, I shall wake you up and send you home peacefully."

Shimon did as the miller suggested. He went to sleep near the Hindu. When he was sleeping soundly, the miller approached him and cut off his beard. Then he took off his hat and put the Hindu's hat on his head. Then the miller woke Shimon, handed him the jug, and said, "I have ground the grain. Go home in peace."

Shimon arrived home looking so strange that Shafika and Rahama were amazed when they saw him. His wife Rahama asked him, "Who are you? Where do you come from?"

Answered Shimon, "I am the husband of one of you, but I do not remember of which one."

"We don't know you," answered Rahama, and she handed him a mirror. When Shimon saw how he looked, he realized immediately that this was not his face. He had never worn a Hindu's hat like that and he always had a beard. Simon shook his head and cursed bitter curses against the miller saying, "That dog the miller! Instead of waking me up and giving me the flour, he woke up the Hindu and sent the flour with him, while leaving me to sleep there. I shall run back to him immediately and ask him to wake me up, because if I stay there and sleep in the heat I might get sunstroke, God forbid."

Shafika turned to Rahama and said to her, "You were right, my friend. I am happy in comparison to you. May the Almighty help you."

·70· *Where Is the Jar?*

IFA 1181. Recorded by Zvulun Kort, as heard in his youth in Afghanistan.

Type 1284, Person Does Not Known Himself (Motif J2012), which also appears as an episode of No. 69 (in this book), "The Two Husbands" (IFA 1749). Another Jewish version of this jest, which appears in A. Druyanov, Vol. II, No. 1061, is told on the stupid people of Chelem; Druyanov includes a reference to an Arab variant. The story is popular in Hungary and is known in India.

• MULLAH NASSER-E-DIN went to the public baths. He washed himself and saw that all the bathers were lying on the floor, rending the ceiling and the sky with their snores. He said to himself: "How good it would be to fall into a sweet sleep!" But what could he do so as not to be exchanged for a neighbor? He took a jar, fastened it to his waist, and fell asleep.

In the meantime one of the sleepers woke up and saw the jar fastened to Nasser-E-Din's waist. He coveted the jar, took it, and fastened it to his own waist. After a short time, Nasser-E-Din arose and saw that the jar was not there. He looked around, and lo! there it was, fastened to the waist of someone else. He woke him up and said, "My friend, if I am I, where is the jar? But if you are me, who am I?"

·71· *What Was the Servant Thinking of?*

IFA 1187. Narrated by Zvulun Kort from Afghanistan, now living in Tel Aviv.

The main motif is J2377, "The philosophical watchman"; Motif

W111.2, "The lazy servant," also present, is always a popular theme in Jewish folklore. Texts belonging to this story-form are classed in J. Balys, No. 2445, "The Serf and the Steward." Versions of this tale have also been recorded in IFA from eastern Europe and Iraq. The origin of thistles is Motif A2688.1.

• A PERSIAN landlord went on a journey. He rode his horse while one of his servants ran ahead of him. By evening they came to a place where they reckoned to stay overnight. After they had eaten their meal, the master said to his servant, "You are tired, as you have been running the whole day; go to sleep and I shall guard the horse until midnight. After midnight I shall awaken you, and you will be on guard while I sleep." The servant agreed and soon fell asleep. The master stood on guard until midnight; then he woke his servant, telling him to guard the horse and saddle. The master fell asleep, and the servant sat down and soon he too was slumbering.

An hour passed. The master awoke and asked, "What are you doing, my servant?"

"I am thinking," answered the servant.

"What are you thinking of?"

"Who sharpened the thistles in the desert?"

"Bravo! You are a good watchman," said the master and fell asleep.

Another hour passed. The master awoke again and asked, "What are you doing, my servant?"

"I am thinking."

"What are you thinking of?"

"Where the dislodged earth goes when a tent is pegged."

"Bravo! You are a good watchman," said the master and fell asleep.

Another hour passed. The master rewoke again and asked, "What are you doing, my servant?"

"I am thinking."

"What are you thinking of?"

The servant answered, "I am thinking that yesterday you rode the horse and I ran ahead. But tomorrow, who will carry the saddle, as the horse is no longer here?"

Glossary

Ashkenazi (pl. *Ashkenazim*) A Yiddish-speaking Jew of eastern Europe; cf. *Sephardi*.

cadi A religious judge (Arabic). According to the theory of Moslem law, the cadi has to decide all cases involving questions of civil and criminal law. However, in practice, only religious problems are brought before him.

Cheder (also *heder*) Old-style Jewish school for boys from seven to thirteen, where they are taught to read the Pentateuch and the Prayer Book in Hebrew.

Eretz-Israel (also *Eretz Yisrael*) Literally, Land of Israel; the Hebrew term for Palestine, occurring in such biblical passages as I Sam. 13:19, II Kings 5:2 and throughout Ezekiel. It appeared in abbreviated form on the coins, banknotes, and stamps of the British mandate government prior to the establishment of the State of Israel. The preference for the term "Palestine" in official usage was resented by the Jews.

galuth The situation of the Jews living in foreign countries, without a land of their own and, hence, subject to persecution and oppression. "Galuth" implies the compulsory banishment of the Jews from the Land of Israel, in contrast to the term "Diaspora" which merely designates the spread of the Jews throughout the world in a more or less voluntary migration. In Hebrew and Yiddish the word is used in a proverb to designate a very long period: *Arokh keorekh he-galuth* (As long as the galuth).

Gamzu ya 'avor "This too will pass." A phrase of consolation uttered in time of misfortune.

gingy Redheaded. Hebrew slang.

haham (also *haḳham, hacham*) A sage. Originally applied to a Pharisaic teacher and later to an officiating rabbi in Sephardic communities. The title "Haham," as used in England, refers to the rabbi of the Spanish and Portuguese congregation in London.

Hasid (pl. *Hasidim*) In early biblical literature, a kindly and benevolent person; in the later literature, a saintly or strictly religious individual. In the Hellenistic period, "Hasid" was used for a member of a Jewish sect that opposed the Hellenization of Jewish life. In modern usage, it refers either to an extremely pious person or to a member of the Hasidic sect founded in eastern Europe by Baal Shem Tov (1700–1760).

hasidei umot ha-olam Righteous gentiles; often applied to non-Jews who, in periods of disaster for the Jewish people, helped Jews escape with their lives from their oppressors.

ḳabbala Originally applied to tradition orally transmitted. In the twelfth century the term was adopted by the mystics to designate the mystical trend and spirit in Judaism.

ḳabil An official in Yemen (Arabic).

ḳohelet The Book of Ecclesiastes.

mashal Parable, fable. In the Bible the term refers to proverbs as well. See I Sam. 24:13 and Prov. 1:1.

Melaveh-Malḳa Literally, "accompanying the Queen," i.e., the Sabbath; actually, the concluding Sabbath meal. Under Hasidic influence the meal is prolonged by singing melodies to delay the end of the Sabbath.

Midrash A body of exegetical literature, illuminating the literal text of the Bible.

minyan The minimum quorum of ten men required for the holding of congregational services. Each of the participants in the minyan has to be at least thirteen years of age. In urban congregations, where it is difficult to assemble ten people for public services, especially on the weekdays, a man is hired to be available for such a purpose. Such a person is called a minyanman.

mitzvah (pl. *mitzvoth*) A commandment, precept, or charge. According to the Talmud (Makkot 23b), there are 613 precepts in the Pentateuch. The mitzvoth are classified in various ways, such as commandments regulating conduct between man and his Maker and between man and his fellows, commandments applicable only to Palestine, and those not depending upon the Holy Land. Colloquially the term refers to any good or charitable deed.

mohel Circumciser.

nargila Water pipe.

nimshal The moral of a parable.

Oved A laborer. A common name in the Bible, as in Ruth 4:17. Here it is given as the name of a hero in a tale from Bulgaria, No. 43, "The Kingdom of the Lazy People" (IFA 423).

pruta A coin of very small monetary value.

Rambam Abbreviation of Rabbi Moshe Ben-Maimon, known as Maimonides, a medieval Jewish philosopher and a famous physician. He was born in 1135 in Cordova, Spain, and left the city in his childhood to escape the Almohede persecutions. After a period of wandering in North Africa and a short stay in Palestine, he settled in Egypt, where he died in 1204 and according to tradition was buried in Tiberias. His tomb, although unmarked, attracts pilgrims to this day.

Rosh ha-Shanah The Jewish New Year, celebrated for two days at the beginning of *Tishre* (in September). It ushers in the ten Days of Penitence, which end on the Day of Atonement.

saddik (pl. *saddiks;* also *tsaddik, tsadik,* pl. *tsadikim*) A term applied to a person outstanding for his faith and piety. In Hasidism the saddik is considered as intermediary between God and man. He gives advice and counsel and offers treatments for illness to his visitors.

seder A religious home or community service; specifically, a ceremonial dinner held on the first evening of Passover (in April) to commemorate the exodus of the Jews from Egypt. Outside Israel the seder is repeated on the second evening of Passover.

Sephardi (pl. *Sephardim*) A west European descendant of Jews from Spain and Portugal, usually darker than an Ashkenazi (*q.v.*).

Shabbat Sabbath.

shalom Peace, the customary form of Jewish greeting.

shed (pl. m. *shedim,* pl. f. *shedot*) A biblical term (Deut. 32:17, Ps. 106:37) signifying devil, evil spirit, or demon. Although the biblical meaning is somewhat ambiguous, in the Talmud *shed* refers exclusively to demons.

shofar A ram's horn blown by the ancient Hebrews as a battle signal (Josh. 6:4–20) and for high religious observances (Exod. 19:19). At the present time it is blown before and during Rosh ha-Shanah and at the conclusion of Yom Kippur.

shohet (also *shokhet, shochet*) A person licensed by the rabbinic authority as a slaughterer of cattle and poultry for use as food in accordance with Jewish religious laws.

Talmud Name applied to each of two great compilations, distinguished as the Babylonian Talmud and the Palestinian Talmud, in which are collected the records of academic discussions and of juridical administration of Jewish law by generations of scholars and jurists in many academies during several centuries after 200 C.E. (A.D.).

tikandi Locked up (Turkish).

toman Persian money.

Torah Traditionally, both the written law given to Moses at Sinai and the oral law, along with every authoritative exposition of the law.

Tsedaka tatsil mimaveth "Charity will save one from death." A biblical phrase (Prov. 10:2) uttered during funeral ceremonies.

vizier Minister of state in Mohammedan countries.

wadi Dry river bed (Arabic).

Yeshiva Jewish traditional school devoted primarily to the study of the talmudic and rabbinic literature. It is a direct continuation of the academies that flourished in Palestine and Babylon in the talmudic and gaonic periods and that were later established in various countries of Europe and on other continents.

Bibliography

AARNE, ANTTI. *See* THOMPSON, STITH.

ABU NA'AMAN (pseud.). *See* SETAVI, MOSHE.

ANDREJEV, N. P. *Type-Index of Russian Folktales* (Russian). Leningrad, 1929.

AUSUBEL, NATHAN. *A Treasury of Jewish Folklore*. New York, 1948.

BALYS, JONAS. *Motif-Index of Lithuanian Narrative Folk-Lore*. Kaunas, 1936.

BASSET, RENÉ. *Mille et un contes, récits et légendes Arabes*. 3 vols. Paris, 1925–27.

BEN-ISRAEL AVI-ODED, ASHER. *Legends of the Land of Israel* (Hebrew). 2 vols. 2d ed. Tel Aviv, 1953.

BEN-YEHEZKEL, MORDECHAI. *The Book of Tales* (Hebrew). 6 vols. 2d ed. Tel Aviv, 1957.

BENFEY, THEODOR. *Pantschatantra: Fünf Bücher indischer Fabeln, Märchen und Erzählungen*. 2 vols. Leipzig, 1859.

BGAZHBA, H. S. *Son of the Deer: Abhazian Folktales* (Russian). Moscow, 1959.

BIN GORION, MICHA JOSEF. *Der Born Judas: Legenden, Märchen und Erzahlungen*. Translated from the Hebrew by RAHEL RAMBERG. 6 vols. Leipzig, 1916–23.

BJAZIROV, A. H. *Ossetian Folktales* (Russian). Stalinir, 1960.

BOLTE, JOHANNES, and POLÍVKA, GEORG. *Anmerkungen zu den Kinder und Hausmärchen der Brüder Grimm*. 5 vols. Leipzig, 1913–31.

BRITAJEV, S., and KASBEKOV, K. *Ossetian Folktales* (Russian). Moscow, 1951.

Buber, Martin. *Tales of the Hasidim, The Early Masters.* Translated by Olga Marx. New York, 1947.

Cahan, Y. L. [Judah Loeb] (ed.). *Yiddishe Folksmayses.* Vilna, 1931.

———. *Yiddishe Folksmayses.* Enlarged and revised ed. Vilna, 1940.

———. *Yiddisher Folklor.* Vilna, 1938.

Campbell, Charles G. *Tales from the Arab Tribes: A Collection of the Stories Told by the Arab Tribes of the Lower Euphrates.* London, 1949.

———. *Told in the Market Place.* London, 1954.

———. *From Town and Tribe.* London, 1952.

Chauvin, Victor. *Bibliographie des ouvrages Arabes au relatifs aux Arabs.* 12 vols. Liège and Leipzig, 1892–1922.

Clouston, William A. *Popular Tales and Fictions.* 2 vols. Edinburgh and London, 1887.

Dawkins, Richard M. *Modern Greek Folktales.* Oxford, 1953.

Dorson, Richard M. "Jewish-American Dialect Stories on Tape," in *Studies in Biblical and Jewish Folklore,* ed. R. Patai, F. L. Utley, and Dov Noy (Bloomington, Ind., 1960), pp. 111–74.

Druyanov, Alter. *The Book of Jokes and Wit* (Hebrew). 3 vols. 5th ed. Tel Aviv, 1956.

Druzhinina, E. S. *Kurdish Tales* (Russian). Moscow, 1959.

Eberhard, Wolfram, and Boratav, Pertev N. *Typen turkischer Volksmärchen.* Wiesbaden, 1953.

Espinosa, A. M. *Cuentos popularos espanoles.* 3 vols. Madrid, 1946–47.

Gaster, Moses. *The Exempla of the Rabbis: Being a Collection of Exempla, Apologues and Tales Culled from Hebrew Manuscripts and Rare Hebrew Books.* London, 1924.

———. *Studies and Texts.* 3 vols. London, 1925–28.

——— (ed.). *Ma'aseh Book: Book of Jewish Tales and Legends.* Translated from the Judeo-German. 2 vols. Philadelphia, 1934.

Ginzberg, Louis. *The Legends of the Jews.* 7 vols. (Vols. I, II, and IV trans. from the German manuscript by Henrietta Szold; Vol. III trans. by Paul Radin; Vol. VII [index] prepared by Boaz Cohen.) Philadelphia, 1909–38.

GROSS, NAFTULI. *Folktales and Parables* (Yiddish). New York, 1955.

GRUNWALD, M. "Spaniolic Tales and Their Motifs" (Hebrew), *Edoth,* II (1947), 3–4, 225–44.

HANAUER, JAMES E. *The Folk-Lore of the Holy Land: Moslem, Christian and Jewish.* Edited by MARMADUKE PICKTHALL. London, 1907.

KABIROV, M. N., and SHAHMATOV, V. F. *Uigur Folktales* (Russian). Moscow, 1951.

KAPIEVA, N. *Dagestan Folktales* (Russian). Moskva-Leningrad, 1951.

KÖHLER, REINHOLD, and BOLTE, JOHANNES. *Kleinere Schriften.* 3 vols. Weimar, 1898–1900.

LITTMANN, ENNO. *Arabische Märchen aus mundlicher Uberlieferung.* Leipzig, 1957.

MARGALIOTH, ELIEZER. *Elijah the Prophet in Jewish Literature* (Hebrew). Jerusalem, 1960.

MEYUHAS, JOSEF. *Oriental Folktales* (Hebrew). Tel Aviv, 1938.

NEWMAN, LOUIS I., in collaboration with SPITZ, SAMUEL. *The Hasidic Anthology: Tales and Teachings of the Hasidim.* New York and London, 1938.

NOY, DOV. "Archiving and Presenting Folk Literature in an Ethnological Museum," *Journal of American Folklore,* LXXV (1962), 23–28.

———. "The Baal-Shem Tov Legend in the Carpathian Mountains" (Hebrew), *Machnayim,* No. 46 (June, 1960).

———. *The Diaspora and the Land of Israel* (Hebrew). Jerusalem, 1959.

———. "Elijah the Prophet at the Seder Night" (Hebrew), *Machnayim,* No. 43 (March, 1960).

———. "The First Thousand Folktales in the Israeli Folktale Archives," *Fabula,* IV, Nos. 1–2 (1961), 99–110.

———. *Folktales in Yiddish* (Yiddish). Jerusalem, 1958–59.

———. "Simpleton's Prayer Brings Down Rain" (Hebrew), *Machnayim,* No. 51 (November, 1960).

OLSVANGER, IMMANUEL. *L'Chayim! Jewish Wit and Humor* (Yiddish). Gathered and edited by I. O. New York, 1949.

OLSVANGER, IMMANUEL. *Raisins with Almonds* (*Rosinkes mit Mandeln*) (Yiddish). Basel, 1921.

PALACIN, A. D. L. *Cuentos Populares de los Judios del norte de Marruecos.* 2 vols. Tetuan, 1952.

PATAI, RAPHAEL; UTLEY, FRANCES LEE; and NOY, DOV (eds.). *Studies in Biblical and Jewish Folklore.* ("Indiana University Folklore Series," No. 13.) Bloomington, Ind., 1960.

PENZER, NORMAN M. (ed.). *The Ocean of Story: Being C. H. Tawney's Translation of Somadeva's Katha Sārit Sāgara.* 10 vols. London, 1923.

RAPPOPORT, ANGELO S. *The Folklore of the Jews.* London, 1937.

SCHMIDT, HANS, and KAHLE, PAUL. *Volkserzählungen aus Palästina.* 2 vols. Göttingen, 1918–30.

SCHWARZBAUM, HAIM. "The Jewish and Moslem Versions of Theodicy Legends," *Fabula,* III (1960), 119–69.

SETAVI, MOSHE (pseud. ABU NA'AMAN). *On the Way to the Land of Happiness: Tales and Legends for Boys, Youths, and Old Men* (Hebrew). Tel Aviv, 1954.

SHEWERDIN, M. I. (ed.). *Uzbekian Folktales* (Russian). 2 vols. Tashkent, 1955.

SIDELNIKOV, W. *Kazakh Folktales* (Russian). Moscow, 1952.

STEVENS, E. S. *Folktales of Iraq.* London, 1931.

THOMPSON, STITH. *The Folktale.* New York, 1946.

———. *Motif-Index of Folk-Literature.* 6 vols. Rev. ed. Copenhagen and Bloomington, Ind., 1955–58.

THOMPSON, STITH, and AARNE, ANTTI. *The Types of the Folktale: A Classification and Bibliography.* ("Folklore Fellows Communications," No. 184.) Helsinki, 1961.

THOMPSON, STITH, and ROBERTS, WARREN E. *Types of Indic Oral Tales.* ("Folklore Fellows Communications," No. 180.) Helsinki, 1960.

Yeda-'Am: Journal of the Israeli Folklore Society. Jerusalem, 1948——.

WESSELSKI, ALBERT. *Der Hodscha Nasreddin.* 2 vols. Weimar, 1911.

———. *Märchen des Mittelalters.* Berlin, 1925.

Index of Motifs

(Motif numbers are from Stith Thompson, *Motif-Index of Folk-Literature* [6 vols.; Copenhagen and Bloomington, Ind., 1955–58].)

A. MYTHOLOGICAL MOTIFS

B. ANIMALS

C. TABU

D. MAGIC

F. MARVELS

G. OGRES

H. TESTS

Q. REWARDS AND PUNISHMENTS

T. SEX

V. RELIGION

W. TRAITS OF CHARACTER

X. HUMOR

Index of Tale Types

(Type numbers are from Antti Aarne and Stith Thompson, *The Types of the Folktale* [Helsinki, 1961].)

I. ANIMAL TALES (1–299)

II. ORDINARY FOLKTALES
A. Tales of Magic (300–749)

B. Religious Tales (750–849)

C. Novelle (Romantic Tales 850–999)

Index of Israel Folktale Archives Numbers

Index of Tales by Country of Origin

General Index

(References to headnotes are given in italics.)

Aarne, Antti (Finnish folklorist), *47, 120*
Abba Hoshaya, 10
Abbas, Shah, 173–75, 78–80, *173*
Abkhazia, *47, 120, 150*
Abraham our Father, 61–62, *93,* 94
Abu Naaman (Israeli writer), *38, 47, 84, 133*
Achikar, Book of, *106*
Adam, 62–64, *133*
Adrianople, Turkey, *130, 183*
Advice, of dying father, 33–34, 57, 66, 113; of old man, 10, 81–83
Affula, Israel, *22, 34, 56, 75, 142, 169*
Afghanistan, 3, 32, 38, 41, 73, 78, 83, 84, 108, 172, 190
Africa, *47, 51, 65, 91, 120,* 139, 140, *152*
Agadic literature, 169. *See also* Midrash
Agnon, Sh. Y. (Israeli writer), *4*
Agriculture, 105
Aharonyan, Elijah (informant), *93*
Al-Bahri, Isaac (informant), *108*
Alkalai, Azarid (collector), *44, 104*
Alkayam, David (collector), *16*
Allah, 98
Almighty. *See* God
America, *139;* Central, *81;* North, *81, 120, 160;* South, *81*
American Indian tradition, *47*
American Negro tradition, *120, 139, 150, 152, 161*
Amrusi, Meir (collector), *85*
Angel of death, 16–18, 31, 40
Animals: grateful, 68–69; language of, 61–62, 79, 160; magic, 5, 46,

153–56; men transformed into, 131–32, 151–52; supernatural being in form of, 25–26, 153–56; talking, 61–69, 154, 158, 160, 162–63; transformed into men, 135, 163–65; ungrateful, 158
Apples, golden, 153–57
Apuleius, *161*
Arab countries, *91*
Arab folktales, *75, 143, 150, 152, 169, 180, 187, 190;* of Lower Euphrates, *126;* Palestinian, *38, 51, 84, 126, 133, 161*
Arabs, 9, *14*
Argentina, *95*
Armenians, *98,* 99–100
Asia, *47,* 139, *161, 187;* central, *4, 31, 46, 51, 78, 109, 113, 143, 150, 153, 161, 180, 183*
Asses, 3–4, 46, 99–100, 135, 181–82. *See also* Donkeys
Avida, Y. L. (Zlotnik), Rabbi, *174*
Avitsuk, Yaakov (collector), *80*

Baal Shem Tov, *4*
Babylon, 15, 65
Baghdad, Iraq, *120,* 185
Baker, 84
Balys, Jonas (Lithuanian-American folklorist), *133, 191*
Baranes, Uri (collector), *31*
Baron, Salo W. (Jewish-American historian), *175*
Barrenness, 16, 18
Bashari, Sara (collector), *117, 157*
Bashari, Zakharia (informant), *157*
Basra, Iraq, *101, 171*